COUNTRY LIVING

COTTAGE *style*

COUNTRY LIVING

COTTAGE

style

MARIE PROELLER HUESTON

HEARST BOOKS

A Division of Sterling Publishing Co., Inc.

New York

PAGE 1: *A TREASURED COLLECTION* of objects becomes an evocative still life on this bedside table.

PAGES 2–3: *SOFT BRUSHSTROKES OF LAVENDER, GREEN, AND BLUE* are sprinkled throughout this serene setting, leading the eye from left to right, top to bottom. The lilac sofa is reflected in the rug and the striped mixing bowl in the foreground. Greens appear in the plant stand, the open shelves of the marble-topped island, and the curvaceous table beside the window. A trail of blue begins with the child's painting on the wall, dips down to coat the tiny chair, then graces the tin picnic basket next to the hydrangeas. Multipaned windows are kept curtain-free, flooding the room with light and allowing an unobstructed view of the yard.

Library of Congress Cataloging-in-Publication Data Available upon request.

10 9 8 7 6 5 4 3 2 1

Book design by Patricia Fabricant

First Paperback Edition 2006
Published by Hearst Books
A Division of Sterling Publishing Co., Inc.
387 Park Avenue South, New York, NY 10016

Country Living is a registered trademark of Hearst Communications, Inc.

www.countryliving.com

For information about custom editions, special sales, premium and corporate purchases, please contact Sterling Special Sales Department at 800-805-5489 or specialsales@sterlingpub.com.

Distributed in Canada by Sterling Publishing
c/o Canadian Manda Group, 165 Dufferin Street
Toronto, Ontario, Canada M6K 3H6

Distributed in Australia by Capricorn Link (Australia) Pty. Ltd.
P.O. Box 704, Windsor, NSW 2756 Australia

Manufactured in China

ISBN-13: 978-1-58816-567-1
ISBN-10: 1-58816-567-1

Contents

Foreword

I've always loved the laid-back style of cottage decorating. Most inspiring for me are the numerous ways the look can be interpreted. During my years at *Country Living*, I've peered inside Adirondack cabins with dark wood paneling and large stone hearths, sunny Southern California bungalows furnished with flea-market finds, cedar-shingled Nantucket dwellings with nautical antiques inside and climbing roses outside, and New York City apartments so authentically "cottage" that if I hadn't known that busy streets lay right outside the windows, I'd have sworn I was in the English countryside.

Just when I think I've seen it all, a creative cottage owner will surprise me by upholstering a wing chair with an old quilt, covering a ceiling with remnants of beautiful wallpapers, or coating a wall with a paint color I'd never have thought to use. All of these inspiring, surprising ideas have been gathered together in *Country Living Cottage Style*. As you flip through the pages of this book, you might fall in love with a room and choose to re-create it down to the smallest detail. Or you might use one of the photographs as a jumping-off point to attempt something similar but with your favorite color, your favorite wallpaper pattern, or your favorite collection. Let your imagination soar!

—Nancy Mernit Soriano
Editor-in-Chief, *Country Living*

OPPOSITE: *Sometimes a single element* can set the mood for an entire room. Here it's the pale apple green of the walls. So pleasing to the eye is this hue that artwork can be kept to a minimum. A set of four floral plates is hung with gallery clips on each side of the window and a framed Victorian engraving is centered over the bed. Classic elements of cottage style throughout the room include the whitewashed iron headboard, the bedding of gingham sheets and floral quilted bedcover, and billowing sheer curtains. The blue-painted side chair adds a single note of deep color to the scene.

Introduction

FILLING A PITCHER WITH FLOWERS highlights its graceful form and imbues a room with cottage style. Here, an ironstone pitcher spills over with delicate pink roses.

For more than two centuries, a cottage in the country has been a romantic ideal in the minds of many people—a picturesque retreat where artists, poets, and everyday folk can escape the worries of the workaday world. One might imagine that to inspire such enduring devotion a dwelling would have to be grand, imposing, and ornately furnished. Quite the opposite is true. For no matter where it's located or what style its architectural elements possess, the cottage is universally humble, cozy, and above all, imbued with an unassuming charm all its own. Clearly, a cottage is more than four walls and the possessions within them; it is a complete seduction of the senses.

The attraction begins the instant the home's exterior comes into view, triggering long-buried memories of fairy-tale houses nestled in forests and sun-warmed kitchens of beloved grandparents. Crossing the threshold, visitors are drawn nearer, beckoned to roam from room to room, to sink into an overstuffed armchair, to inspect the treasures filling the dining-room hutch, or to rest beside a bright windowsill and watch butterflies flutter through the flower garden. Nowhere else are the seemingly incongruous emotional states of serenity and joyful expectation as artfully conjured.

We can thank the British aristocracy of the eighteenth and nineteenth centuries for sparking the Western world's love affair with the cottage. It was this group of people who first recognized the intrinsic beauty of the simple dwellings inhabited by country craftsmen, merchants, and farmers. Many wealthy landowners commissioned architects to design similar living quarters—often replete with such classic details as thatched roofs, ivy-covered walls, and latticework windows—for their gardeners, gameskeepers, and coachmen. One-room cottages even became common garden elements akin to gazebos and hedge mazes, providing a country gentleman with an idyllic spot to retire to for an hour or so.

As the nineteenth century progressed, the cottage became a symbol of the slower-paced rural way of life that was increasingly threatened by the advancements of industrialization, adding a nostalgic glow to the small structure's growing popularity. Across the Atlantic, Victorian America embraced cottage style with the same fervor with which it greeted anything pertaining to hearth and home. Not only did the Victorians appreciate the buildings' aesthetic qualities, they also admired what they perceived to be the moral virtues of these modest houses. "What an unfailing barrier against vice,

immorality, and bad habits," opined landscape designer Andrew Jackson Downing in his 1842 book, *Victorian Cottage Residences,* "are those tastes which lead us to embellish a home whose humble roof, whose shady porch, whose verdant lawn and smiling flowers, all breathe forth to us a domestic feeling that at once purifies the heart and binds us more closely to our fellow beings!"

The final element that ensured the cottage's perfect fit with the American way of life was its small scale, a factor that made acquiring a home of one's own an accessible, affordable dream for the nation's burgeoning middle class. Architects gleaned ideas from home and abroad to create efficient, attractive designs: Colonial-style Cape Cods, Carpenter Gothic farmhouses, and English stone cottages to name a few. One style in particular, the Arts and Crafts bungalow, was so popular

ALTHOUGH MOST COTTAGE GARDENS feature a veritable patchwork of colorful blooms, some homeowners choose one beloved flower and plant it in profusion. Hydrangeas were the blossom of choice for this cottage owner. A patch of grass and breathing space between each hydrangea bush keep the look from overtaking this small plot.

A PERFECT EXAMPLE OF mismatched elements coming together to create an inviting whole, this headboard and bedside table work together beautifully. The scalloped edges of the pillowcase complement the gracefully turned legs of the side table. The milk glass lamp dates from the 1930s.

during the first two decades of the twentieth century that its columned veranda and broad roof were among the most common sights in suburban areas developed during that era. Ladies' magazines of the day helped spread cottage style throughout the land. Such publications as *Good Housekeeping* and *Ladies' Home Journal* taught homemakers how to outfit interiors in the casual style that best suited cottage living. Furnishings were comfortable and durable, never fussy or difficult to clean. Colors were subdued, upholstery prints and dinnerware patterns pretty. Treasured collections filled cupboards and crannies. And gifts from nature, be they potted plants, dried herbs, or fresh flowers from the garden, provided a finishing touch to the homey scene.

Little has changed in the past hundred years. Twenty-first-century interpretations of cottage style still exude comfort, casualness, and a penchant for pretty things. There are, however, a few major differences between then and now. For one thing, it's no longer necessary to live in a cottage to enjoy the home's myriad charms. Upholstering a city apartment's sofa with an exuberant cabbage-rose print, positioning an iron bed frame in the guest room of a suburban split-level ranch, or arranging a collection of framed botanical prints on one wall of a lakeside cabin will instill laid-back cottage spirit in each of these dwellings. Another difference is that homeowners today sprinkle a healthy amount of humor into this old-fashioned decorating style. Hang a crystal chandelier in a country dining room? Incomprehensible a century ago. Now whimsical combinations of patterns, colors, textures, and materials abound.

Country Living Cottage Style salutes

both traditional takes and fresh twists on this enduring look. On these pages, you'll visit dozens of homes and glimpse countless notions. We'll highlight essential elements that make a room "cottage," showcase everyday interiors transformed into charming oases by their creative owners; and provide tips on choosing the best cottage-style furnishings, reviving secondhand finds and displaying cherished objects throughout the house.

To TRANSFORM A TINY MUDROOM into the charming breakfast area shown here, walls and floors were whitewashed and simple wooden side chairs were painted an irresistible shade of blue. The drop-leaf table can be pushed against the wall when not in use. Blue mixing bowls rest on top of a cupboard-turned-pantry; the tall beaded-board piece holds canned goods, table linens, and kitchenware. A white braided rug greets dirty feet by the doorway without breaking up the clean look of the floor. Garden flowers arranged in a blue-and-white enamelware pitcher add the perfect finishing touch to the country scene.

1

Living Rooms

PRECEDING PAGES: *GENEROUS COATS OF CREAM PAINT* were applied to pine paneling to make this living room appear more spacious. The shade of green chosen for the bookshelves, mantel, and trim matches a favorite collection of plates now displayed on the wall and also complements the yellow and chartreuse furnishings. Framed botanical prints, potted plants, and floral-motif pillows attest to the owner's passion for gardening. Family photographs and heirlooms like the 1930s mirror above the fireplace are scattered around the room. When the owners first moved in, wall-to-wall carpeting covered the home's original chestnut flooring. A good sanding and an application of polyurethane brought the floors back to life.

"Have nothing in your houses that you do not know to be useful, or believe to be beautiful." Never do Arts and Crafts reformer William Morris's words seem more significant than when considering the cottage and, more specifically, the cottage living room. Usefulness is of the essence here. Although space is limited, guests should be as graciously accommodated as possible. Beauty cannot be overlooked either, for as the most public room in the house, the living room should be a repository of your favorite things—objects that reveal your personality, your pastimes, and your passions.

Before a single piece of furniture can be brought in, the room itself must be analyzed. Look first at your walls. What color would best suit the space and best complement your collections? For many cottage owners, some variation of white (pearl, eggshell, cream) is the color of choice. Not only do white walls make small spaces appear larger, they also offer no contrast or competition to the furnishings or objects placed against them. (No wonder they're so common in art galleries.) For others, though, all white seems a bit cold. These people might choose a barely-there shade of blue, yellow, gray, or sage green. Pale hues still make a room feel bigger and might even accentuate deeper tones of sky blue, ocher, charcoal, or hunter green found in the furniture.

By and large, paint is used more often than wallpaper in cottage living rooms because of space constraints. When papering is chosen, however, prints tend to be tiny or softly colored. Hanging wallpaper above wainscoting or beaded board paneling is one way to keep a lively print from overpowering a room. Turn your attention next to floors

EVEN THOUGH THE LIVING ROOM in their lakeside retreat was decidedly cozy, the owners wanted plenty of comfortable seating for guests. Their solution was to position two overstuffed sofas on either side of the room; crisp white slipcovers keep the large furnishings from overpowering the small space. An ottoman serves triple duty as footrest, coffee table, and additional seating. Built-in bookcases flank the river-stone hearth, providing much-needed storage. The tops of the bookcases were aligned with the mantel, creating one long shelf on which to display a collection of black-and-white photographs.

and windows. Cottages with wonderful old pine, oak, or maple floorboards are highly admired. Most homeowners keep wood floors uncovered and lightly polished, taking care to protect high-traffic areas with runners in hallways and area rugs in front of sofas and beneath dining tables. Other people prefer to cover floors, perhaps opting for wall-to-wall sisal or a plush carpet in a cheerful color. Woven and hooked rugs, whether genuine antiques or new pieces made in the traditional manner, work especially well in cottage living rooms because they can reflect colors and textures found elsewhere in the room. Windows, too, can be handled in a number of different ways. Shades and shutters create a streamlined look; lace curtains or floral-motif draperies match more exuberant interiors.

While there are certain furnishings that typify the cottage look, no

LEFT: *THIS BRIGHT, AIRY BEACH COTTAGE* is as casual as they come. Yet the owners still managed to inject a few elegant details into the scene, such as the grand gold-framed mirror over the sofa and the blue-and-white porcelain vase on the side table. Whitewashed walls and bare floors visually expand the room's limited space. Shelves hung between exposed wall studs support a healthy supply of books, games, family photos, and other mementos. A lift-top pine trunk positioned beneath the window serves as extra storage as well as a charming window seat when topped with a cushion and pillows.

ABOVE: *ALTHOUGH THIS COLORFUL COTTAGE* is located in California, its owner filled it with reminders of her childhood spent in New England. Homey plaids and rustic details abound—the deer head, paintings of outdoor scenes, and curtains made out of old woolen camp blankets, for example. The floor and beaded-board paneling were painted white to balance the bold swatch of plaid along the top of the walls. A mixture of new and vintage fabrics upholsters the sofa, armchairs, and pillows. The unifying factor among all objects in the room: adherence to a strict color scheme of red, green, and gold.

particular style need be excluded from this type of decorating. A classic interior usually includes an overstuffed, slipcovered sofa and one or two matching armchairs. These items work well because they are extremely comfortable, easy to care for, and seem to extend an immediate

RIGHT: *RECORD-ALBUM COVERS WERE USED* as templates for the ceiling's collage of plaid and floral wallpapers. When hanging art on the walls, be creative: In addition to traditional paintings, trays or plates bearing similar motifs work just as well.

invitation to all who pass by to sit down and relax. Rustic furnishings that capture the spirit of the great outdoors also work well in the cottage living room. Homeowners who love the rustic look have been known to flank a fireplace with Adirondack porch chairs or to position a wicker rocking chair beside a plant-stand-turned-side-table. If more formal designs appeal to you, don't despair: Graceful wood-framed settees and slipper chairs upholstered in chintz can work just as well. Many people even enjoy combining casual and formal elements into a cohesive whole.

Once the furniture is in place, collections are the next detail to ponder. Beloved objects can either be incorporated into more practical arrangements (like bud vases beside a row of garden books) or given a space all their own, such as an entire cupboard filled with ironstone or a

curio cabinet filled with figurines. Mantels are particularly good places to showcase possessions because they are an area of the room the eye is naturally drawn to. A wonderful collection of books, too, should be given a place of honor in the cottage living room. Built-in bookcases are a desirable feature in a room, but if your home lacks this detail, alternatives include a standing bookcase, a hanging shelf, or a short glass-front design. Piles of art books can also be placed around the room on tabletops (ideally beside a comfortable chair) so guests can flip through them at their leisure. If your book collection is large enough, you could even create a small table beside a sofa or chair by piling broad volumes one on top of the other.

The finishing touch to the cottage living room is artwork on the walls. In a typical English cottage, framed prints of botanical studies, historical events, animals—especially dogs—and domestic scenes often covered walls in a haphazard manner. Today, displays tend to be sparser—highlighting a single row of botanical prints, for instance, or a small cluster of silhouettes. The area above a mantel is a natural place for a large painting, print, or photograph. Landscapes, marine paintings, floral studies, and animal portraits are all popular choices for this space. Walls over a sofa can be daunting to fill: Try a row of three or four similarly framed prints (botanicals or Currier and Ives-style images, for example) or an arrangement of family photographs in frames big and small. Sometimes hammer-shy homeowners choose not to hang up anything at all. In such cases, artwork can be lined up on a mantel or side table, creating visual interest without pounding one nail into a wall. The choice is entirely up to you.

OPPOSITE: *Viewed individually,* the components of this stylish sitting room might seem too different to work well together. What makes them click is their complementary color scheme of bold reds and golds set against a whisper-blue backdrop. The tactile quality of the furnishings—vintage-fabric pillows, timeworn worktables, and weathered architectural elements—also unites these seemingly disparate objects. To balance the rich textures in the room, walls are kept clean by placing paintings on tabletops and along the floor. An old wood box and a wire basket are stored under the tables to keep warm blankets and children's toys out of sight when not being used.

MIXING AND MATCHING FABRICS

Layering different fabric patterns can energize a room, but avoiding a look that's too busy can be tricky. To begin, choose a complementary color scheme (red and white or blue and white, for example) to unify varying prints like toiles, plaids, and stripes. Limit yourself to one or two dominant hues in a single setting—such as the red and purple seen here—to prevent overpowering arrangements.

BELOW: *EVERY COTTAGE NEEDS* an over-stuffed armchair for its owner or honored guest to flop into and relax. Plush pillows and a soft, warm throw are also essential to attain the most comfortable position and to ward off any unwelcome drafts. Hatboxes covered in ticking stripe provide clever and attractive storage.

ABOVE: *BLUE AND WHITE* is one of the most popular color combinations of all time—and it's easy to see why. Fresh stripes cover sofa and armchairs in this sunny living room. Pillows made from vintage ticking-stripe and a checkered tablecloth add a touch of old to the new. A painted garden bench runs the length of the double window, keeping beloved books and collections within easy reach. Above the window, a peg rail becomes a whimsical and unexpected curtain rod. Minimally adorned white walls and a whitewashed floor covered with a woven rug contrast the dark wood ceiling.

24 ❦

Slipcovered Furniture

The benefits of slipcovers in the home are many. Foremost among them is that these easy-to-care-for covers allow you to have elegant pieces of furniture positioned prominently in the living room, swathed in the colors and patterns you love, without having to worry about random spills or children's sticky fingers. Just zip off the outermost layer of fabric and into the wash it goes—that's what makes slipcovers such an essential part of casual, comfortable cottage style. Another plus is the fact that slipcovers fashioned from the same pattern, color, or family of colors can unify different styles of sofas, armchairs, slipper chairs, and ottomans, creating a harmonious look without having to spend extra money for a matching suite of furniture. Changing only the slipcovers is also a budget-conscious way to give a room a whole new look. Likewise, keeping an extra set of slipcovers on hand allows you to dramatically alter the mood of a room depending on the season. White covers add seashore style to a home in the summertime; hunter green or deep red covers look wonderfully warm and cozy around the holidays. Slipcovers made from a large, single sheet of fabric (available through a number of mail-order catalogues these days) work well if you want to try a new look just for a season, as these options are simple to drape on any sofa and are less expensive and easier to store than a full set of slipcovers.

Most decorating sources offer custom slipcovers from their upholstery departments. If you are in the market for new furniture, bring swatches of the drapery pattern or paint color with you so you can choose a complementary fabric. Keep in mind that certain fabrics are easier to care for than others. Cotton twills and denims are the most worry-free, since these can be put in the washing machine. Damasks and velvets will likely require dry cleaning. If looking to order new slipcovers for furniture you already own, the same stores can usually send an upholstery expert to your home to take measurements and make new slipcovers in a matter of weeks. A third option (for sewing aficionados only) is to make your own slipcovers. Craft books available in bookstores lead you through the entire process, from choosing the best fabrics to using the proper weight needles and thread.

OPPOSITE: COLLECTIONS HAVE BEEN PARED DOWN and colors turned up a notch to create this elegant twist on the cottage interior. Striped upholstery fabric continues the room's clean lines without forfeiting comfort. A pier mirror with a wide wood frame leans against the wall, visually expanding the space. On the mantel, a large framed photograph and three smaller landscapes make a pleasing, condensed arrangement. A tiered metal stand in the corner elevates everyday items—tin buckets, a gazing ball, and a wire basket—to works of art by allowing viewers to see their sculptural qualities.

RIGHT: IF SPACE PERMITS, invite guests to peruse your book collection by placing favorite titles out on a table. Armchairs covered in the same soft lavender fabric as the drapes stand nearby, while a leather ottoman stashed neatly beneath the table can be brought out in a flash whenever a footrest or additional seating is needed. A potted orchid, fresh roses in a crystal vase, and a bowl of potpourri introduce elements of nature in the indoor setting.

Window Seats

Whether your goal is time alone with a cup of tea and a new novel or quality time with young children and a picture book, few spots in the home are as inviting as a window seat. From this cushioned perch, you can look into the room and absorb all the comforts of home. You can also gaze into the garden or out onto a bustling street and let your mind wander as far as it wishes to go. If your home does not already have a window seat, adding one will ensure hours of enjoyment for you and your family.

Bay windows are perhaps the most natural spots to transform. Owing to the bay window's shape, a seat can be constructed without using any extra space in the room, a plus in small dwellings. Standard windows can also become window seats, but placement here will require a little planning if the seats are to appear as they most often do—as if set into the wall. A simple way to achieve this much-loved style in front of a standard window is to build wide bookshelves on either side, leaving space for a seat in between. Although this design eats up a bit more room space, the additional bookshelves make up for it: You can never have too many bookshelves in a cottage interior.

Carpenters (or handy homeowners) can easily take window and room measurements and purchase wood for the project at a local lumberyard. Be sure to design your window seat with storage space in mind. Underseat storage (accessible either by a lift top or cabinet doors facing the room) is an ideal spot for toys, board games, and sports equipment. For a seamless appearance, paint the window-seat's frame to match the trim color in the room. A window seat in a room with white trim, for example, looks best when painted white; a seat in a room with green trim will look lovely in a matching shade of green. As a finishing touch, order custom slipcovered cushions from an upholstery shop near you. Fabric patterns that match existing drapery or sofa covers are a good option. Another choice would be a solid hue that complements other furnishings in the room.

This room's sofa, armchairs, and footstools all vary somewhat in style. To make them look like a matching set, the owner upholstered them in cream and yellow damasks that complement the pale lemon-yellow of the walls. A built-in cupboard beside the fireplace houses a large collection of transferware. When elegantly framed and hung over the mantel, a poster of a folk-art portrait takes on the look of a genuine antique for a fraction of the price. The arrangement beside the doorway is easy to reproduce: Position a favorite side chair and hang two (or more) framed prints, photographs, or mirrors in a column above it.

LEFT: *THE SPIRIT OF THE ADIRONDACKS* lives in this rustic cottage. Furnishings, fabrics, and collections all honor the great outdoors. A colorful camp blanket softens the leather couch while an early 1900s indigo-and-white quilt hangs over the back of the rocker, ready to fend off the evening chill. A collection of old juvenile series books (including the adventures of Tom Swift and others) is housed in a weathered bookcase, adding to the room's atmosphere. A thirteen-star American flag fills open wall space and instills patriotic flair.

OPPOSITE: *A CHARMING DUTCH DOOR* opens onto the living room, a space dominated by a dramatic stone hearth. The owners replaced the fireplace's original circa 1960s brick face with large flagstones. They also removed a dropped ceiling, revealing the original crossbeams and giving the room a more open, airy feeling. A row of pewter tumblers filled with fresh garden flowers lines the mantel, adding a delicate touch to the stately hearth.

ABOVE: *WOOD PANELING AROUND THE FIREPLACE* was painted the same shade of yellow as the living room walls. The color complements a collection of Ohio pottery vases and a 1930s flower painting discovered at a flea market. The ceramic deer head on the wall adds a whimsical touch.

OPPOSITE: *THE BOLD CARPET PATTERN* supplies a solid base for the living room's mixture of furnishings. A low-arm sofa piled with pillows, matching upholstered armchair and ottoman, and high-back Mission armchair provide plenty of seating.

PROFILE ❧

A Cottage Decorated with Antiques

When two antiques collectors decided they'd had enough of New York City's hectic pace, their search for a country retreat led them to Bucks County, Pennsylvania, a rural oasis only a few hours from the Big Apple. Here, amid rolling hills and quaint villages, the collectors happened upon a 1926 Craftsman-style cottage. Though modest in size, the house featured plenty of windows, original woodwork, and a fireplace surrounded by antique tiles from the Moravian Tile Works in nearby Doylestown, Pennsylvania. It was a perfect match, and the new owners lost no time transforming the interior into a suitable backdrop for their extensive collections of pottery, furniture, textiles, and more.

They turned their attention first to the walls. Instead of wallpaper, the owners chose paint in solid, soft colors that would allow their precious possessions to be the center of attention. For the living room they chose a warm yellow that took on an extra glow once the room's red, tan, and cream furnishings were put in place. In the dining room, a pale blue was chosen to ground the table, chairs, and accessories painted in deeper shades of red, green, and blue. The kitchen's deep-olive walls and cream woodwork emphasize the intimacy of the small space. The exposed beam ceilings throughout the first floor were whitewashed to create an open, airy atmosphere.

While color reigns on the first floor of the house, white walls prevail on the second floor, where the bedrooms are kept crisp white, making the cozy quarters tucked under the eaves feel a bit more spacious. White walls also add a sense of serenity to the bedrooms, which are intended very much as respites from the public areas of the house.

LEFT: *IF THESE MIXING BOWLS* had been relegated to a kitchen shelf, their exquisite colors and patterns would have been far less noticeable. The circa 1900 painted cupboard and single framed watercolor against the pale-blue wall keep the arrangement's look simple and elegant.

Amplifying the coziness of the upstairs rooms, patchwork quilts and plush pillows dress the beds. Enticing piles of books are arranged on tabletops and, space permitting, inviting armchairs are placed beside sunny windows.

Windows and floors in the house were handled in opposite ways. Windows throughout remain curtainless. Instead, the owners chose shades to keep the line from floor to ceiling clean and unfussy. (Unadorned windows also allow a maximum of sunlight to enter the space and offer unobstructed views of the garden.)

Floors are quite another matter: Underfoot, color and pattern were given free reign to run wild over the floorboards. Hooked rugs in classic patterns and flat carpets in bold botanical prints add visual interest to a part of the house that is often overlooked. With the stage set, the

RIGHT: *New rush-seat chairs* and a grand-father clock made from salvaged wood combine with antiques and curios. The circa 1960 hooked rug reflects all the colors found in the room. The shades are affixed to the bottom of the window, letting in sunlight while still providing ample privacy. Tin ornaments were turned into shade pulls at the windows.

owners added their furnishings and collections to the scene.

Although pieces in their collection come from different periods and different geographic regions, their common threads are color and craftsmanship. An appreciation for fine construction has also led the owners to purchase creations by contemporary craftspeople working in traditional methods. New and old, antique and vintage, all items are mixed and matched to create an interior that is a thoroughly livable home, not a museum.

As with all successful cottage interiors, comfort is key. Children are always welcome, the owners' two dogs are free to roam, and guests can collapse onto the sofa and put their feet up without a moment's hesitation. The way the owners arrange their collections throughout the cottage is worthy of note as well. First, objects are often

LEFT: *Butcher-block countertops*, old-style iron cabinet hardware, and a hooked rug add country flair to the tiny kitchen. Modern appliances don't seem out of place when kept sleek black below the counters and all white above. Artwork and objects are sparingly arranged.

OPPOSITE: *THIS BRIGHT BEDROOM* proves that even the smallest spaces can be turned into charming sanctuaries. Red-and-white vintage linens (including a Robbing Peter to Pay Paul quilt) dress the twin bed. A tiny closet, a few good books, and a single painting and lamp complete the scene.

removed from the area for which they were originally intended. For instance, late-nineteenth- and early-twentieth-century mixing bowls are taken out of the kitchen and placed on top of a painted cupboard, allowing guests to focus on (perhaps for the first time) the range of color, pattern, and shape to be found. Elsewhere in the house, a child's toy rests on a kitchen shelf, and a painted workbench supports metal garden ornaments in the dining room. Another tactic is grouping items by theme—size, shape, or color—which effectively increases the visual impact of a collection. This can be seen in the mixing-bowl arrangement as well as the selection of colorful vases positioned on the mantel. When displayed in unexpected spots or an out-of-the-ordinary manner, cherished objects catch visitors by surprise and bring a smile to their faces.

ABOVE: *SAGE-GREEN SHADES* add a touch of color to the all-white bedroom and complement similar hues seen in the sheets, blankets, and accessories. The leather armchair and stately Mission oak bed frame share the same warm tone. Remnants of a crazy quilt became a cover for the ottoman.

RIGHT: *A GARDEN BENCH* stripped of paint now supports books beside a bright window. The leather armchair and upholstered ottoman with flattened ball feet create a cozy spot that invites hours of reading enjoyment.

2

Kitchens & Dining Areas

Before the cottage became an established architectural style, kitchens in homes of taste were situated away from the public areas of the house; in many cases, stowed away in the basement or in a separate structure altogether. At the time, cooking odors that permeated the house were a homemaker's worst nightmare. Over the years, the stature of the kitchen has grown. The compact size of the cottage home may have had something to do with it. Without ample space for an off-site or basement-level room, cottage kitchens were integrated into the first-floor layout. Placed at the back of the house and afforded plenty of windows for cross-ventilation, the kitchen soon became a favorite family gathering place. Nowadays, even dinner guests love to linger here while the host and hostess prepare the food. (Small wonder, then, that upholstered armchairs have become a common sight in the kitchen. A wing chair in the kitchen would have confounded the nineteenth-century homemaker!)

To assess the cottage potential in any kitchen, you must first analyze the available storage space. Because square footage can often be limited, be sure there are ample cabinets and shelves for everyday dinnerware and kitchen collectibles like tin canisters, enamelware coffeepots, and Jade-ite mixing bowls. Ample cabinet space is key. In older homes that lack period cabinetry, new designs with an old-fashioned look can be purchased or commissioned from a cabinetmaker. If all-new cabinets strain your decorating budget, give common wood cabinets an antique look by painting (white or any color) and gently distressing with sandpaper. Many devotees of the cottage style opt for glass-front

THE SPIRIT OF SUMMER CAMP fills every corner of this cabin's kitchen. A refurbished refrigerator from the 1940s is flanked by a retro-style stove in tomato red and an early 1900s cupboard that's been given a fresh coat of soft-green paint. Left unpainted, the wood paneling and exposed beams add to a room's coziness. When it comes to displaying collections, the owners take a strict "the more, the merrier" stance: Printed tablecloths are stacked on a shelf and hung from a wall rack, Jade-ite mixing bowls line the top of the cupboard while other Depression-glass designs fill its shelves. On the wall, a plate rack with remnants of original green paint hangs beside a farm-stand sign.

cabinet doors to showcase china and glassware. Others dismiss cabinets altogether and instead build open shelves throughout the room to display collections and everyday wares for all to see.

Once you've assessed the storage situation, turn your attention to the colors that will coat walls and woodwork. Light hues open up tight spaces, which explains why white and pale pastels are so common in the cottage kitchen. You might decide to keep the walls white and paint the cabinetry and woodwork blue or green. Or perhaps the walls should be sunny yellow and the cupboards glossy white. Details like window treatments, sinks, flooring, furniture, and lighting fixtures will further personalize your kitchen.

Do typical English cottages appeal to you? If so, your kitchen might feature lace at the windows,

a deep soapstone sink, tile floors, and an ornate gas lamp (converted to electric) suspended above a round oak table and chairs. If a 1940s Cape Cod is more to your liking, try gingham curtains, a double porcelain sink, linoleum flooring (yes, it is still made), and a chrome-and-milk-glass lamp over an enamel-topped table and chrome-and-vinyl side chairs. Even a modern aesthetic can find its way into the cottage kitchen in the form of industrial pendant lamps, stainless-steel appliances, and a pared-down, uncluttered look.

Another reason the eat-in kitchen's importance has increased in the cottage home is the fact that when floor plans do include a separate and distinct room for formal dining, the space is frequently usurped for use as a home office or extra bedroom. In homes where the dining room can be used for its original purpose, consider making it

OPPOSITE: *In this seaside cottage,* one corner of the open living-dining-cooking area has been designated the dining room. The marvelous sculptural table and mismatched seating prove that many variations of wood can work well together in a single setting. Wood furnishings also allow the sunny yellow walls and sea-blue waves outside the curtainless windows to provide the room's primary colors. A collection of straw hats displayed on a delicately curved coatrack combines artistry with practicality. The narrow column between window and door is filled with a selection of cherished objects, including plates, a painting, and an antique clock. Oak floorboards are kept carpet-free to underscore the space's clean lines. Easy sweepups are an added bonus to bare floors in a beachside home.

RIGHT: *When decorating this colorful space*, the homeowner sought to re-create the kitchen of her youth. A toned-down shade of turquoise (a classic 1950s color) brightens the breakfast area and echoes the kitchen's cheerful striped wallpaper. Decorative paint techniques were added to the walls (light sponging produces a cloudlike texture) and the floor (a trompe l'oeil cat stretches playfully on a checkerboard pattern). Vintage-fabric curtains pick up the yellow from the floor design. Despite their varying shades of yellow, blue, and green, similarly styled side chairs work as a set. A comfortable armchair is upholstered in vintage printed tablecloths and ticking stripe; the table beside the window was made by stacking a blue bed tray on top of a blue garden bench.

as grand as possible, though never ostentatious. Position a tall hutch with a timeworn painted surface or a warm wood stain against the wall and fill it with your favorite set of china, the rose-patterned teacups you inherited from your grandmother, or knickknacks collected over the years. Table and chairs can be casual and grand at the same time: Consider a farm table (as long as will comfortably fit) flanked by two long benches and topped with a tower of shiny apples in a repurposed garden urn, or a whitewashed round table, toile seat covers on whitewashed chairs, toile drapes at the window, and a beautiful flower arrangement in a cranberry-glass vase. In rooms where furnishings are colorful and patterns busy, keep floors clean and simple by choosing sisal carpeting or a woven rug in neutral tones. Boldly patterned rugs stand out in rooms with toned-down furnishings.

OPPOSITE: *PALE LEMON-YELLOW WALLS* and bright white trim create a cheerful atmosphere in this breakfast area. Open shelves above the windows support a collection of floral-motif plates and platters. Three favorite plates are hung with gallery clips to bring visual interest to the far corner of the room. A cabinet unit built out into the room delineates cooking and dining areas and provides additional display space for milk-glass compotes. The small stool comes in handy when dishes need to be retrieved from their roosts or if a third person will be sitting at the table. Because the rest of the room is clean lined (no curtains, bare floors), the slightly worn surface of the white-washed table and mismatched plank-seat side chairs goes virtually unnoticed.

ABOVE: *IDEAS FOR USING OLD ITEMS* in new ways abound in this welcoming kitchen: Tea towels have been transformed into curtains that coordinate with the soft-green walls, a garden urn holds utensils in the center of the room, baskets in a cubby beside the sink can hold table linens or dry goods, a vintage chalkboard becomes a reusable surface for shopping lists and phone messages, and coat hooks hold colanders and tea towels on the wall. Plus, a hamper turned garbage can proves that trash receptacles don't always need to be hidden away under the sink. Open shelves display a collection of ironstone pitchers and a lovely set of brown-and-white transferware. To increase work space without limiting floor space, the owners chose a narrow work island; mixing bowls and serving pieces are stored on the open shelf below.

A *WIDE ANTIQUE SINK* is the focal point of this sunny kitchen. Outfitted with gleaming new fixtures and a fresh porcelain finish, the large piece features drainage shelves on both sides of the sink. A collection of white ironstone pitchers parades along the sill of the double window, while other ironstone items occupy an open shelf high above. Open shelves elsewhere in the room also provide easy access to a floral-motif tea set, bluebird porcelain canisters, cookbooks, and homemade preserves. A barely-there shade of yellow coats cupboards, and old-fashioned glass knobs and drawer pulls add sparkle throughout the space. A vintage hooked rug bearing a bold flower design adds color and pattern to the floor.

Breakfast Nooks

Humble in purpose and size, breakfast nooks are one of the easiest parts of the house to make exquisitely pretty. True breakfast nooks are just that—nooks or alcoves turned into dining spots in space-deprived kitchens. Some feature built-in banquettes with a table in the center, while others accommodate a small table and freestanding chairs. Today we use the term breakfast nook more loosely to describe any dining area in a cozy kitchen, whether tucked behind a counter or beside a window. Any small table—square, round, or rectangular—will work here, although whitewashed wood and vintage enamel-topped styles seem especially well suited. Banquettes, short benches, or four-chair sets are all good seating options. Other choices include garden chairs, bistro chairs, or mismatched designs unified by a coat of the same color paint. Window coverings can be old-fashioned in feeling (eyelet or gingham curtains) or more modern (whitewashed wooden blinds or no curtains at all). On the table, printed tablecloths from the 1950s with colorful fruit or flower motifs or checkered designs in red and white, blue and white, or yellow and white look great. Keep fine china in the dining room and instead bring out your sturdiest ironstone or everyday china bearing floral patterns or simple stripes of cobalt around the edges. For a finishing touch, arrange garden flowers in a pale-blue canning jar or coffee tin.

Anyone wanting to create an alcove for a breakfast nook in a kitchen that has none can enlist the help of a carpenter, cabinetmaker, or handy spouse. Start in a sunny corner of the room—ample light is essential for a nook you'll want to linger at all morning with newspaper and coffee. If space is tight, consider building a wall that is flat on the side facing the corner you want to enclose. Line the other side of the wall (the side facing out toward the kitchen) with floor-to-ceiling shelves to create extra storage space for dishes, cookbooks, tin canisters, and accessories. If space permits, you might even consider building a small pantry in place of a wall of shelves. Budget-conscious people can avoid construction costs by positioning a large hutch where the wall would be, facing its back toward the dining area and its shelves toward the kitchen.

IN KITCHENS WITH AMPLE SQUARE FOOTAGE, work islands become indispensable elements. Beaded board on the sides of this sizable example mirror the wall treatment throughout the room; its sage-green hue, however, gives it a personality all its own. The decision to place the sink in the island also opened up sunny counter space beneath the windows. Glass-front shelves in the island protect cookbooks, mixing bowls, and cake plates. Glass doors also grace the dramatically tall hutch, where collections of yellowware and ironstone share shelf space. Everyday china is kept within easy reach in the open plate rack to the right of the fridge. Well-worn wood tables like the one in the foreground are great for potting plants and arranging flowers.

ABOVE: *In kitchens that lack sufficient cabinet space,* large cupboards are essential for storage. Both antique designs and newly made pieces can be found in a range of sizes and colors to suit your home. Storing flatware in small pots and tumblers is a terrific way to show off their decorative handles.

OPPOSITE RIGHT: OPEN SHELVES are great places to display china and glassware in the kitchen. But don't feel you need to confine one material to one shelf—such as all stemware on one shelf, for example, and all ceramics on another. This lively grouping combines ironstone, transferware, crystal, copper molds, and an antique wooden potato masher.

RIGHT: LET YOUR KITCHEN REFLECT YOUR INTERESTS. Enthusiasm for gardening and collecting led this owner to choose a fern-print wallpaper and an elegant whitewashed display shelf with towel bar that can showcase favorite pieces, from a basket collection to a linen collection.

OPPOSITE: *WHIMSICAL DETAILS* such as the chandelier combine with traditional pinks and greens to bring a touch of romance to this dining room. The table's "tea cozy" cover and the seat cushions were created from a vintage-style quilt and coordinating floral fabric. A little paint can work magic: The hot pink chairs, fifteen years old, have been painted at least twenty times and the armoire is repainted whenever the room takes on a new identity.

DECORATING WITH CHANDELIERS

Chandeliers can add a gleeful touch when hung in a casual setting. Dining tables in particular need ample lighting, and chandeliers are a natural choice. Although glimmering crystal is not unheard of, more classic designs include painted toleware in a floral motif, Scandinavian-style ironwork, and graceful brass with cloth shades. Many old chandeliers can be electrified and antique lamps rewired.

Dutch Doors

Dutch doors have been a common sight on American farmsteads for centuries. Although the origin of the term is foggy (some trace it back to the Netherlands, others to the Pennsylvania Dutch community), the meaning is the same: Dutch doors are divided horizontally so that the upper and lower parts can operate independently of each other. In the farmhouse, these doors were often found in the front or back doorway. Opening the top of the door would air out the house while maintaining a certain level of privacy and keeping out unwanted critters. With the top open, doors with a small ledge atop the bottom door provided comfortable spots to lean on while talking with neighbors and passersby.

Dutch doors were also used in stables; opening the top would ventilate the stall without setting the livestock free. In today's cottage home, these doors are used most often as back or side doors that open onto a garden or porch. They are especially useful in a kitchen, as leaving the top of the door open will draw out heat and cooking odors while keeping pets inside (or outside, as the case may be). Dutch doors can also be positioned in interior doorways. Opening only the top of a door can be helpful in kitchens, home offices, and studios at times when you want to hear what's going on in the rest of the house but would prefer pets and small children to stay out.

A fortunate few may discover original Dutch doors in cottage homes. In these cases, a fresh coat of paint may be needed to restore the door to its previous glory. Antique examples sometimes surface at shops specializing in architectural salvage. Bring the doorway dimensions with you when you begin your search, as old doors are sometimes wider than modern doorways. Although the majority of home-improvement stores do not include Dutch doors among their regular stock, most can special order them for you. Prices will likely be higher than standard doors, so calculate the cost into your decorating budget.

Carpenters and cabinetmakers may be able to construct a new Dutch door or to turn an existing door into a Dutch door complete with new hinges and hardware. If a craftsperson does not have his own blueprint, check how-to books in your local bookstore or conduct a Web search for door designs on home-improvement sites.

RIGHT: *A PASSION FOR ANTIQUE PAINTED FURNITURE* with timeworn surfaces prompted the owners of this kitchen to apply a distressed finish to all cabinets and woodwork in the room. Floor-to-ceiling shelves protected by glass doors put china, glassware, and an extensive collection of green pottery on display. Positioning a mirror over the range as a backsplash gives the room added depth. The countertop plate rack is a handy detail. A lovely piece of botanical-motif ironwork turns a ho-hum range hood into a focal point of the room.

LEFT: A LARGE COLLECTION OF JADE-ITE inspired the color choice for this kitchen's walls and work island. To break up the large expanse of white cabinetry, drawer fronts and cabinet-door trim were painted green. Thick butcher block was chosen to top the island, while white tiles cover counters throughout the room. A retro-style double lamp with a delicate edge adds a hint of whimsy to this clean-lined setting. A vintage picnic basket kept beside the island is always ready for impromptu outings.

OPPOSITE RIGHT: *ATTENTION TO DETAIL*
saves this all-white setting from blandness.
Woodwork around the windows has been
painted a cream that's a shade darker than
the walls. A blue chair back adds a touch of
color, and slight scuffing on chairs and table
adds texture.

ABOVE: *An OLD-FASHIONED BREADBOX* adds
a touch of cottage to any kitchen. Here, both
the enameled breadbox (a flea-market find)
and the vase are color coordinated with the
collection of Jade-ite dishes, teacups, and
saucers. A sense of unity is created by keeping
the background color white and accessorizing
with one or two predominant colors.

ABOVE: *A FRESH TWIST ON BOOK DISPLAY*: Volumes are stacked on their sides, creating eye-catching columns in the living room. A collection of Victorian paintings lines the top of the bookcase (roses were a favorite subject for amateur artists in the nineteenth century). When displaying collections, whether still-life paintings or green vases, grouping a few great pieces together heightens the visual impact.

OPPOSITE: *TO CREATE THE PLEASING MANTEL-TOP ARRANGEMENT*, clusters of collections were placed on both sides of a family portrait (mercury glass on one side, green McCoy pottery on the other). The mantel was custom built for the space and is a reproduction of an antique design spotted at a Paris flea market. The armchair rocker was a $25 tag-sale find; new beige-and-white striped slipcovers gave it a new lease on life.

A Cottage Decorated with White

The hectic pace of daily life slows to a well-deserved stand-still when the owners of this 1911 Seattle cottage return home. Inside these doors serenity reigns. One of the main reasons the interior is so calming to the senses is the palette of white-on-white used throughout the house. Some people might fear that focusing on all white might limit their decorating possibilities. But as this dwelling proves, there are plenty of opportunities to experiment, play, mix, and match within the world of white. For one thing, there is no single shade of white. Rather, the color family includes pure white, pearl, eggshell, ecru, and many other variations. Add just the slightest dab of green, blue, yellow, lavender, or gray and you've created a whole new range of nearly imperceptible shades that read as white when on the wall. Textures, too, can liven up a neutral scene:

Layering white cotton and damask, whitewashed wood and metal, and cream-bodied ceramics will result in a look that is anything but ordinary.

In this cottage living room, walls have been kissed with a hint of beige while molding, bookshelves, and mantel received generous coats of bright white. Two overstuffed sofas face each other in front of the fireplace; washable cotton slipcovers ensure that everyone—including the owners' lively Jack Russell terriers—is welcome. Bare floors and pared-down collections emphasize the room's clean lines. White accessories mindfully placed around the room include the diminutive side table, alabaster lamp, and glass-topped coffee table (originally a garden piece). Although the furnishings, collections, and accessories come from different places and different periods of time, all exude comfort and beauty in their own

LEFT: *To prepare the dining room* for a special luncheon, trails of ivy were laced through the tole chandelier and the standing candelabra. On the table, etched-glass goblets and flower-pattern plates top a delicate lace tablecloth; the dog figurines are a favorite collectible of the home's animal-loving owners. A colorful bunch of garden flowers provides the perfect centerpiece.

OPPOSITE: *A pale shade of mint* coats walls in the guest room, where an elegantly carved and painted Victorian bed frame is dressed with romantic floral-patterned linens. A painted cupboard safeguards the belongings of overnight guests and supports a simple yet strong arrangement of antiques: a garden urn turned flower vase, a nineteenth-century still life, and a blown-glass footed bowl filled with beaded fruit. In the hallway, a plush love seat and books piled on an upholstered ottoman demonstrate how easy it is to convert a cozy corner under the eaves into a comfortable reading room.

way, making them seem like perfect matches.

A small alcove off the living room was turned into a garden-inspired dining room. Talk about maximizing space: You'd be hard pressed to pack more decorative details into a room twice this size. Folding French garden chairs pull up to a painted Swedish table. An Italian tole chandelier full of cheerful daffodils floats over the table, while dramatic, standing candelabra stand at the ready for candlelit suppers. A 1920s hooked rug brimming with leaves and blossoms continues the botanical theme underfoot. At the window, thick velvet caramel-colored drapes frame a verdant garden scene. Because the drapes, the toleware, and the hooked rug make such a bold visual statement, the dining room needs no artwork on the walls.

Strong proponents of saving a home's original architectural elements whenever possible, the owners were pleased to find period cabinetry still intact in the kitchen. A fresh coat of paint and new drawer pulls and brass latches with an old-fashioned style breathed new life into the nearly century-old cabinets. Behind the glass doors, green- and blue-glazed mixing bowls and other pottery pieces were carefully arranged to showcase the breadth of the collection while keeping the overall look of the shelves uncluttered. Industrial details including pendant lamps, gray painted wood floors, and poured concrete countertops are scattered throughout the low-tech space, keeping the kitchen from becoming too quaint for the owners' more contemporary taste.

A healthy dose of quaintness does reach the bedrooms, however. In these spaces, bed frames chosen for their graceful curves and wonderfully worn surfaces are piled high with pillows, ruffle-edged shams, and thick down comforters. It's all a visitor can do to resist jumping in and curling up for a long nap. This is precisely the reaction the owners want to elicit with their simple style of decorating in the bedrooms and all through the house. Their home is an escape, a place where life's simple pleasures—a good book and a comfortable chair, a delicious meal shared with friends, a warm bed that begs to be napped in—are to be savored.

RIGHT: *A GARDEN OVERFLOWING* with flowers and foliage is a natural extension of the cottage home. Here, the rainy Pacific Northwest climate helps roses, daffodils, and bluebells thrive. To decorate this outdoor "room," garden statues, including ceramic ducks and a cement cupid, have been placed in the flower beds.

3

Bedrooms

PRECEDING PAGES: *To keep MULTIPLE PATTERNS* from overwhelming a room, determine the dominant color in most of the prints and then add a few solid blocks of that color to ground the look. In this cheerful bedroom, red was chosen as the unifying color and has been used to coat the shutters, the writing desk and chair, and the low bench at the foot of the bed. Vintage textiles offer out-of-the-ordinary alternatives to standard room accessories: A yellow-and-white checkerboard quilt has been transformed into curtains while yellow fabric lampshades trimmed with red rickrack and ruffles make mismatched lamps look like a perfect pair. The playful four-poster bed is an ideal choice for this setting.

Although every inch of your house should reflect your interests and your own sense of style, the decoration of most rooms will occasionally take other people's needs into account. Is there ample seating for guests around the dinner table? Is there enough space on the coffee table for visitors to rest their drinks? The bedroom, however, is the one place that is entirely about you. This is the room in which you dream, in which you greet each new day. Passions for roses or lace or even frilly hats that may be toned down elsewhere can be set free here. Conversely, more modern sensibilities can continue their reign by choosing simple patterns and understated furnishings.

In keeping with the scale of the house, most cottage bedrooms of the late nineteenth and early twentieth centuries were small and many were tucked right up under the eaves. For this reason, light colors and diminutive patterns on wallpaper and sheets (rosebuds, for example, or thin stripes) were most common. Furnishings, too, were generally pared down to the barest necessities. In the smallest bedrooms you'd often find only a bed, a nightstand, and a dresser. Where space permitted, larger pieces were added: an armoire, a small writing desk and chair, a blanket chest, an armchair and reading lamp. Floors were generally kept bare, with an area rug positioned beside the bed. At the windows, simple lace, eyelet, or sheer curtains did the trick. Decorations on the walls were also kept to a minimum, consisting only of a mirror over the dresser and a single framed painting or print.

More than a century later this image of the cottage bedroom remains clear in our minds. Paying attention to these details—small patterns, light colors, delicate textures, and simple decorations—is the secret to translat-

BEDDING PATTERNS need not match when colors do: On this bed, stripes, florals, checks, and solids are unified by their blue-and-white color scheme. The same colors extend to the woven rug on the floor and the quilt squares over the cast-iron headboard. When framed, unfinished quilt squares make great wall decorations. Examples from the early 1900s have an old-fashioned feeling and are also extremely inexpensive, rarely selling for more than a dollar apiece. (Squares from the nineteenth century, on the other hand, sometimes fetch much more when antique prints are of interest to fabric collectors.) Apothecary cabinets, like the one visible behind the door, can be fun and practical accessories in all-white rooms.

ing cottage style into bedrooms of all architectural styles and geographic locations, be they city apartments, suburban homes, or grand estates.

Once a decision has been made regarding the walls (paint versus wallpaper), the most important thing to focus on is the bed because it will set the tone for the room. Iron beds have an undeniably old-fashioned appeal. Sleigh beds are for true romantics. Upholstered headboards can match curtains or furnishings; the type of fabric can make the room ultra-feminine (a large cabbage-rose print) or more modern (a bold stripe). Trundle beds are great for kids' rooms because they make even the smallest space sleepover-ready. No matter what style of bed frame you choose, bedding should be irresistible: crisp sheets, a pile of soft pillows, and a wonderfully textured quilt or plush duvet.

If closet space in your bedroom is not what it should be, additional storage is advisable, not only for clothing but also for extra blankets, stationery, photo albums, hatboxes, or what have you. Armoires are natural choices and can either reveal bare wood or a surface painted to match the room's decor. Imagine a white-washed armoire against soft-green walls, a polished pine model against a wallpaper pattern of tiny red rose-buds, or a blue-painted cupboard that perfectly matches cheerful blue-and-white gingham sheets.

Because its size can sometimes dominate a bedroom wall, plan displays of art or collections around an armoire. For a symmetrical arrangement, hang similarly themed prints (botanical subjects work especially well) on each side. For a more casual look, you might hang three floral plates on one side using gallery clips and position three vintage photographs vertically on the other side. The tops of armoires are also great places to display

RIGHT: *THIS SUNNY BEDROOM* shows just how easy it is to instill a city apartment with cottage spirit. Start with a romantic bed—in this case a carved-wood and cloth headboard—and dress it with linens and quilts and plenty of pillows. Next, hang something delicate at the windows, such as the chambray half curtains seen here. (For extra privacy, a shade could be installed without affecting the window's neat look.) Choose a few favorite items for the wall and hang them in a casually askew manner, such as the black-and-white photographs of Paris and floral platter between the windows. Finally, add a luxurious detail (maybe a small writing desk like the one at the foot of the bed) and bring a bit of the natural world indoors by lining potted plants along the windowsill.

collections like baskets, McCoy vases, or painted wood hat stands. If an armoire is not part of your bedroom plan, cluster artwork over the bed or dresser, or hang a few favorite pieces between windows or doorframes. "Cluster," of course, will mean different things to different people. It may be a row of three gold-framed pansy still lifes in a simply styled lavender room or a collection of a half-dozen equine paint-by-numbers over a desk. When choosing art for bedrooms, don't be afraid to look beyond standard art forms like paintings, prints, photographs, and drawings. Hooked rugs with house-and-yard scenes or animal motifs can look great when mounted on the wall, as can baby quilts or trade signs with appropriate themes like "No Vacancy" or "Sweet Dreams Motel."

BELOW: *WITH AN ARCHITECTURAL ELEMENT* as striking as this window, a small bedroom under the eaves needs little else in the way of decoration. Simple furnishings in this room include a graceful cast-iron bed, a small table, and a side chair. Even the floor is unadorned. The blue blanket chest adds a dash of color and provides extra storage for bedding and guests' belongings as well.

ABOVE: *RECENTLY IT'S BECOME COMMON* to see frames—just frames—hung on the wall for decoration. When displayed in this manner, the distinctive designs of these utilitarian objects are easier to appreciate. The simple frame in this country bedroom mirrors the clean lines of the four-poster bed, the peg rail, and the exposed beams above.

OPPOSITE: *AN ORNATE BED FRAME* is the focal point of this tiny bedroom. Wooden garden furniture like the armchair seen here makes an easy transition indoors when painted white and given a comfortable, boldly striped cushion. A collection of minia-ture seascapes surrounded by frames made of salvaged wood flanks the closet door.

Quilts

Intricately stitched and beloved by generations, quilts are among the clearest symbols of comfort in American culture, making them a natural choice for the cottage interior. While the pastel palette and romantic pattern names (Grandmother's Flower Garden, Double Wedding Ring, Sunbonnet Sue) of Depression-era quilts complement traditional cottage furnishings particularly well, nearly every design from any age can find a home here. Two-tone creations from the nineteenth century, such as indigo-on-white Flying Geese or red-on-white School House patterns, appear with frequency, as do bold floral appliqués from the 1940s and '50s.

One advantage to twentieth-century quilts is that they tend to be a bit sturdier than delicate nineteenth-century quilts, a plus if you intend to use and display them in a bustling household. New quilts—either from a department store, a boutique, or your own sewing machine—are generally the easiest to care for, as their fabrics are stronger and more colorfast than those used in the past. By and large, new quilts can be popped into the washing machine (gentle cycle, mild detergent) and dryer (low heat) if they get soiled. Many people choose to clean antique and vintage quilts before displaying them directly on beds, sofas, or tabletops. Older quilts should be hand washed, rolled in towels, and laid flat to dry because their stitches and fabrics can become weak or damaged with excessive movement.

Dressing a bed is one of the most common ways to display quilts in the cottage home. Bear in mind that if the bottom of the bed is a favorite napping area for a family cat or dog, you may want to purchase a coordinating throw or blanket that can be placed over the bottom of the quilt during the day. The habits of house pets should also be taken into account if a quilt is to be displayed over the back of a settee, folded atop a blanket chest, or draped over a wooden quilt rack. Stacking quilts in a country cupboard is a wonderful way to showcase favorite designs safely. Although hanging quilts on walls has become quite popular in recent years, a cottage's size can affect the process. Ideally, quilts hung on a wall should be up off the floor by at least six inches to avoid a buildup of dust. Attractive alternatives for small spaces include mounting crib quilts or quilted wall hangings. Be sure to keep wall-mounted textiles out of the line of direct sunlight, which can cause fading over time.

FOR RENT
2 Bed Room Cottage
WITH
FURNISHED KITCHEN
BY NIGHT OR WEEK

DARK COLORS ARE UNCOMMON in cottage bedrooms. But as this navy oasis proves, they can work just fine when done right. The first rule is to keep bedding at the same intensity as the walls. For example, if the sheets, pillows, and comforters in this photograph were all white or delicate florals, the dark walls would seem as if they were closing in. Dressed with bold linens like these—saturated blues and reds specked with white—the beds and walls complement each other. A single graphic sign on the wall breaks up the large expanse of blue.

OPPOSITE: *WHITEWASHING THE WALLS* and rafters of this uninsulated summer cottage created an airy sleeping loft. A portion of picket fence was used to make a one-of-a-kind headboard. Flea-market finds in the room include the small dresser, the hunter-green wicker side table, and the whitewashed porch chair. Family photographs and vintage snapshots line the ledge beside the window. An extra quilt folded at the foot of the bed adds color to the all-white space.

ABOVE: *HAND-PAINTED FURNITURE* was a staple of the Victorian cottage bedroom. Wooden bed frames, small dressers, and bedside tables are among the most common items found in today's antiques market. This pair of twin beds was made in Austria in the early 1900s. Their new owner crafted matching duvet covers using a coordinating rose-motif fabric she found in a quilt shop. To apply old-fashioned floral motifs to new furniture, consult craft books on stenciling and decorative painting techniques in your local library or bookstore.

RIGHT: *SOMETIMES PEOPLE LOOK* to collections to determine the direction of a room, like choosing paint for the walls a shade lighter than a favorite yellowware bowl or selecting brown-and-white toile curtains that mirror a display of brown-and-white transferware on the wall. This colorful bedroom is a Roseville vase (foreground) come to life. Exposed brick walls were painted a cheerful lilac. Amateur still lifes line a crackled-paint bureau while long chromolithographs are hung above the bed. The height of the bookshelf along which the Roseville vases are resting adds privacy to the bed—a great idea for studio apartments where living and sleeping quarters share one space.

ABOVE: *FLEA-MARKET AND THRIFT-SHOP FINDS* are perfect for bedrooms in summer cottages where the goal is often to accommodate as many guests as possible with minimum financial expense. White sheets and matching woolen blankets make these mismatched twin bed frames work as a pair. The cheerful yellow bedside table has just enough surface area for a reading lamp, books, and a bouquet of garden flowers. The standing globe adds visual interest and also acts as a conversation piece for guests. The narrow ledge above the beds can be used as display space for tiny vases, family photos, and seashells.

BELOW: *EVEN THE SIMPLEST ITEM* can make a big impact in a cottage bedroom when you learn to spot the decorative potential in everyday objects. Take a wooden chair like this one, for instance. If you'd spotted it at a flea market with a weathered surface and no seat, you might have walked right past it. Add a pretty new upholstered cushion and it becomes an attractive accessory beside a window or in front of a writing desk. Vintage straw hats, too, might seem to be of no use to those who aren't fond of wearing hats. But even a single one can add an instant feeling of a garden party to any room. Hanging two or more along a peg rail or on a wire coat rack enhances the appeal.

ABOVE: *AN ANTIQUE TYPEWRITER* in working condition serves both decorative and utilitarian purposes when set on a side table in a bedroom. Most amateur paintings and antique prints found at flea markets are inexpensive. Grouping a selection by theme (in this case, country scenes) can help achieve a pleasing arrangement with little cost or effort.

LEFT: A *SIGNIFICANT BENEFIT* of cast-iron bed frames is that they often can be maneuvered into the tiniest of bedrooms. What's more, their airy quality means that even queen-size frames like this one won't overwhelm small spaces. The strong lines of this frame are echoed in the iron curtain rod above the window and the folding stool at the foot of the bed (a detail that would make a great luggage rack as well). Wall-to-wall sisal carpeting, butter-yellow walls, plush pillows and quilts, and a reading chair upholstered in white soften the straight lines of the room's metal accessories. Leaded-glass doors add an elegant touch; search for similar designs at flea markets, salvage shops, and antiques malls.

Cast-Iron Bed Frames

A sheer curtain flutters in the breeze by an open window, a transferware ewer and basin rest on a bureau, and a cast-iron bed frame supports a patchwork quilt and a pile of pillows. These are some of the timeless images of the cottage bedroom, and central to this mental picture is the bed frame. Part of the allure of cast-iron beds is the range of styles that can be found, from extremely simple to gracefully curved. The fact that light and air flow through these frames—as opposed to a mahogany sleigh bed, for instance— means that you can place one in a very small bedroom without worrying that it will overpower the space.

The decision facing each cottage decorator with an eye for a cast-iron bed is whether to buy a new frame, readily available these days through home- design stores and mail-order sources, or to search for an antique? New frames often appeal to busy people because they can offer the old-fashioned look that's wanted in the exact color and size desired with a minimum of fuss. This is especially convenient because queen- or king-size frames can be difficult to find on the antiques market. One drawback to new frames is that they can be pricey, a fact that leads many people to scour antiques malls, flea markets, and country auctions in hopes of finding a perfect specimen from the past. Most old frames on the market date from the late nineteenth and early twentieth centuries, when the style was widely used in summer cottages throughout the country. Value will generally depend on age (more recent examples tend to be less expensive), degree of detail, and painted finish (white is common; soft blue and green are especially desirable). Although some buyers covet a well- worn painted finish, many choose to refinish antique frames either by hand or by hiring a professional furniture restorer. This is probably a wise decision if the frame is intended for a child's room, as most of the paints used years ago were lead- based. A fresh coat of paint can even make two frames with slightly different designs look like a perfect match—a plus when decorating a child's room, vacation home, or guest room.

LEFT: CANOPIES ARE AMONG THE MOST ROMANTIC BEDS, but the scale of cottage bedrooms sometimes makes them impossible to fit in. A simple drape of sheer or lacy fabric is a wonderful solution, capturing the feeling of a canopy in even the smallest of spaces. A length of fabric and a simple hook or peg are all that's needed to create this look. The graphic floor pattern is an unexpected yet whimsical addition to the room. A similar pattern could be painted onto a wood floor or achieved with common kitchen tiles.

ABOVE: LAYERING COLLECTIONS and furnishings of the same color adds dramatic yet understated texture to a bedroom. In this serene setting, the dresser, hall mirror, and beaded-board paneling have all been whitewashed. Onto this backdrop, cherished objects are carefully arranged: an ironstone footed bowl, a McCoy vase, and a vintage alarm clock.

BELOW: WHEN COTTAGE BEDROOMS lack ample storage space, armoires prove extremely useful. In addition to storing clothing and extra blankets, they can artfully hide televisions and stereos. When painted the same color as the walls (here it's white on white), even large pieces can blend seamlessly into the closest of quarters.

ABOVE: ORNATELY CARVED VICTORIAN BEDS can be irresistible. But the dark woods that were commonly used during that era can sometimes overpower small cottage bedrooms. To lighten dark wood frames like the pair of twin beds in this photograph, choose sheets and blankets in cool shades of white, blue, and green. Plaids and ginghams work especially well. Clusters of small framed prints or photographs on the walls and unassuming garden bouquets (this arrangement fills a blue canning jar) also help add a casual feeling to formal furnishings.

OPPOSITE: *This restful guest room* was created with limited fuss and minimal funds. To color coordinate the space in an instant, walls were painted a soft lavender-blue, a few shades lighter than the prominently placed periwinkle-blue lamp. Because both are white, mismatched twin bed frames look like a pair. Chenille bedspreads with pom-pom fringes and ticking-stripe pillows on each bed emphasize symmetry. On the wall, two whitewashed wood shelves hung close to each other support a lovely collection of floral-pattern porcelain; the antique mirror adds height to the arrangement. A 1930s hooked rug placed between the beds injects a touch of bold color and pattern to the airy scene.

GOOD IDEA

DECORATING WITH PLATES

Decorative plates look great on the table, but they can also be wonderful solutions to bare walls throughout the house. Group plates by color (brown-and-white transferware or Jade-ite, for example) or theme (such as roses or violets), then center them, smallest (at the top) to largest if they vary in size, over a chair, small desk, or side table to keep the look elegant. Gallery hooks, available at art-supply stores, work well for larger arrangements; ridged art shelves give single plates or short rows of plates an air of importance.

A Fieldstone Cottage

Nestled amid tall hemlocks beside a fishing creek in northern Pennsylvania, this 1906 stone cottage boasts a natural setting that is truly idyllic. The interior of the rural hideaway, however, presented its new owners with a challenge: Would they be able to instill a sense of warmth and comfort to rooms with austere stone-and-mortar walls? The answer, as you can plainly see, was yes.

The first thing to be done was to choose a color scheme that would enliven the main living areas. Deep, rich shades of red and green seemed like a natural choice for woodwork, window frames, and exposed beams to brighten the space. Interior window trim was coated with a warm rust-red that takes on a rosy glow when illuminated by sunlight or candlelight. Exposed beams and paneling in the living room were painted an unusual shade of green

that falls somewhere between hunter and sage. The effect is stunning, leading the eye upward and around the room.

Living room furniture was upholstered in similar variations of red and green. Matching armchairs and ottomans flank the stately hearth; the sofa's red-and-green floral pattern is barely visible beneath a colorful patchwork quilt and numerous velvet and needlepoint pillows. On the floors, Oriental carpets continue the theme of color and texture underfoot. Although the dwelling reflects the requisite ruggedness of an Arts and Crafts design, the owners' collection of Colonial-style furnishings and accessories brings refinement to the rooms. This is most evident in the dining room, where reproduction Windsor chairs surround a Queen Anne table. A carved mahogany mirror on the stone wall and a gracefully curved pewter

OPPOSITE: *Luxurious fabrics on furniture*, throw pillows, and floors add to the warmth of this living room. The dramatic presence of the stone hearth is accentuated with a single painting in an elegant gold frame. Forced bulbs, like the tulips in matching rustic wood containers, awaken the magic of springtime in the heart of winter. When not used on the dining table, a collection of silver napkin rings makes an eye-catching arrangement in a red bowl on the coffee table. Other everyday objects that look great when grouped together include cookie cutters, thimbles, and New Year's noisemakers.

ABOVE: *A glowing centerpiece* adds springtime spirit to this winter table. To re-create this look in your own dining room, place forced bulbs in a country basket in the center of the table and surround with votive candles.

chandelier over the table enhance the look.

Delicate touches can also be found in the bedrooms, though both Colonial and Arts and Crafts aesthetics are left far behind here. The predominant style in bedrooms is Swiss chalet, houses in which polished pine paneling often covers walls and ceilings, and crisp white linens dress comfortable beds. The contrast between the main areas and the bedrooms is striking, yet it works because both exude a rustic country sensibility.

Because space is limited in the cottage, making the most of storage was a priority. Cupboards, dressers, and blanket chests inside the house store collections, clothing, and household accessories. A wooden shed behind the house was an essential addition for the storage of items that can weather fluctuations in temperature and humidity (dry

goods; folding chairs for extra seating; and sets of sheets, towels, and blankets can be kept here). Among the most important items in the stone cottage's shed are pieces that help both owners and guests fully enjoy each season of the year. Sleds and cross-country skis are kept on hand for snowy pursuits; fishing rods, inner tubes, gardening supplies, and patio furniture appear when the warm weather arrives. A coat of blue paint that coordinates with the exterior woodwork on the house creates the feeling of a small compound of buildings.

Bathrooms 4

PRECEDING PAGES: *A SINGLE SIDE CHAIR* set beside a classic claw-foot tub holds all the necessities for a relaxing soak. Side chairs are useful accessories in the bathroom; in addition to toiletries, they can hold towels, magazines, or a potted plant without taking up much space. Shaker-style peg rails above the beaded board are another wonderful detail. Pegs can be used for practical items (to hold a towel, for example) or purely decorative ones (like the lovely landscape shown here). Shelves set into the wall provide extra storage space. Notice how the towels on the shelves pick up colors found elsewhere in the room.

Bathrooms as we know them today—separate rooms featuring sink, toilet, and tub—were a rarity when cottage architecture first reached our shores in the nineteenth century. Back then, kitchen sinks, copper bathing tubs set beside a fireplace, and outhouses fulfilled a family's various hygienic needs. As the twentieth century dawned and cottages became a common style for suburban homes, the bathroom became a symbol of the modern American lifestyle. Manufacturers of the day began to design coordinating sinks, tubs, and toilets appropriate for both grand and modest homes. While outhouses would remain common sights at vacation cottages well into the 1900s, no town residence was considered fashionable without a distinct bathroom.

From the start, homeowners began beautifying this utilitarian room. Women's magazines offered ideas for pretty curtains, wall stencil patterns, hooked rugs, and framed prints and photographs. Even today, bathroom remodeling articles are among the most popular features in home-design magazines. Perhaps the small size of the room lets homeowners feel free to experiment with colors and patterns they might consider too bold for other rooms in the house. There are so many ways to approach decorating the cottage bathroom. One of the most classically old-fashioned looks involves beaded-board paneling on the bottom half of the walls with soft pastel paint or a tiny floral-print wallpaper above. Ideal accessories for such a room include a claw-foot tub, a pedestal sink, and wispy curtains made of eyelet or gingham. A darker, more Victorian feeling could be created with hunter-green walls and matching curtains and sink skirt fashioned from a strong pink-and-

RIGHT: VANITY TABLES ARE DESIRABLE DE-TAILS, but many cottage homeowners think the table-and-chair sets cannot fit into small rooms. As this photograph illustrates, however, even modest bathrooms can accommodate a vanity if they are well designed. A narrow ledge with drawers, cabinets, and space for a diminutive wooden stool was planned along one wall of this sunny bath. A thin mirror was positioned between the windows; a lamp hung above the mirror provides additional lighting for makeup applications. Sea-green floor tiles add a dash of color to the all-white room.

LEFT: *When combined*, white walls and marble counters and floor tiles bring elegance to any bathroom. Large mirrors (or two mirrored doors set side by side like the ones seen here) visually expand small spaces. Thick white towels accentuate the clean look of the white and gray room.

underfoot when placed in front of the sink or beside the tub or shower; solid colors can coordinate with curtain fabric or wallpaper pattern while hooked or woven rugs can add a nostalgic touch to the room.

Storage is an important consideration in cottage bathrooms, especially when undersink cabinets or linen closets are not large enough. If you have a freestanding sink whose base you do not mind covering up, a sink skirt can create ample space with minimal fuss. Simply choose a fabric that coordinates with the colors or patterns already found in the room, then hem all sides and stitch one side of Velcro tape to the top, facing front. Using epoxy glue, attach the other side of Velcro to the inside top of the sink, then press the two parts together. Baskets are another quick, attractive way to expand storage space in the bathroom. Magazines, towels, washcloths, and extra rolls

RIGHT: FREESTANDING SHOWERS are luxurious details in bathrooms that can accommodate them. Even though most cottage bathrooms will be too small for a shower of this scale, some homeowners choose to refurbish an extra room or even add onto the house to create the bath of their dreams.

of toilet paper can all be stylishly stored here. Even chairs, stools, and narrow plant stands can become additional bathroom storage. Set beside the tub or window, they can gracefully support stacks of towels or wire baskets filled with toiletries.

To decorate bathroom walls, choose works of art that will not be damaged by humidity and occasional splashes of water. Framed botanical prints can be a nice look here, as can framed Victorian advertisements for soaps, tooth powders, and face creams. Seashore themes work particularly well in the bath, so feel free to frame vintage engravings of seashells or watercolors of coastal scenes. To emphasize a room's overall theme, coordinate collections with art—seashells and beach glass in a room with nautical art, for example, or a selection of nineteenth-century cold-cream jars beneath Victorian beauty advertisements.

Antique Sinks

Your bathroom can be new from floor to ceiling—sparkling white tiles, delicately striped wallpaper, gleaming brass towel holders—yet if you install an antique sink, the room will instantly radiate an authentic old-fashioned aura. No wonder these items are so eagerly sought by decorators, collectors, and restoration experts. Ask any architectural salvage source or antiques shop in your area, and they'll tell you that antique sinks are hot commodities, and when they appear, they're snapped up quickly. But don't despair, new models appear regularly, so you won't have to wait too long to find your perfect match. Examples from the not-too-distant past (the 1930s and '40s) are appearing with greater frequency these days and generally cost less than late-nineteenth- and early-twentieth-century examples.

Many styles of sinks can work in the cottage bathroom. The most classic is the pedestal sink. Within this style are numerous variations, from extremely sleek designs to those that are more curvaceous. The style you choose will likely depend on the other details of the room. Curving forms will complement more romantic takes on the bathroom; sleek sinks will fit a more modern decor. Another good choice for a more contemporary vision of the cottage bath is a deep double sink, originally found in kitchens and laundry rooms. These can be a fun change from the standard his-and-her sink. In country bathrooms, some creative owners have even been known to transform moderately sized farm tables or work tables into one-of-a-kind sinks by carving a hole in the top and resting an antique basin in the resulting space.

To find the sink of your dreams, scour architectural salvage stores, antiques shops, or flea markets. Antique sinks even appear on Web auctions from time to time. If you don't see the exact style you want right away, show dealers a picture of what you're looking for and ask them to keep an eye out for you. Many will be interested in the offer, will take your number, and will call you if and when they find a match.

With all antique bathroom items—sinks, tubs, or toilets—chances are good that you'll need to resurface the porcelain and replace the fittings. Fortunately, a number of companies make plumbing fixtures based on antique designs, and many sell directly through nationwide home-improvement stores. Enlist the aid of a plumber or general contractor to return your piece to its original glory.

BELOW: *To ADD COLOR AND TEXTURE* to the bathroom, one crafty homeowner transformed a chenille bedspread into a shower curtain. In addition to chenille bedding, cotton camp blankets, colorful quilt tops, and graphic bark cloth would also work well. Before hanging, hem all sides of the fabric and reinforce the holes along the top with grommets. Choose a coordinating shower-curtain liner in clear, white, or colored vinyl to protect the fabric from splashing water.

ABOVE: *DRAMATIC DETAILS* make strong statements, even in tiny bathrooms. In this powder room, a thick mahogany frame surrounds the mirror while figural sconces grace the walls. White walls, white towels, and a blowsy white curtain keep the rest of the space airy, while a few favorite beach finds along the windowsill add texture to the scene.

ABOVE: *COORDINATING COLLEC-TIONS AND WORKS OF ART* is an easy way to create a cohesive look in any room. In this vignette, a fish sculpture with folksy flair is displayed above a bowl filled with gifts from the sea.

OPPOSITE: *FURNISHINGS LIKE THE GRASS-GREEN SOFA* and blue-painted coffee table provide punches of color in the white-walled sitting room. A similar faux fireplace and mantel can be created using molding and hand-painted decoration inside the frame. Garden furniture is a natural fit for the cottage home: A pair of whitewashed wicker chairs flank a wicker table in the sitting room while a 1950s metal patio chair brightens the hallway.

A Cottage Alive with Color

Most people are a bit timid when it comes to using bright colors and bold graphics in the home, especially in the cottage home, where space constraints generally dictate light colors and delicate patterns. Not so the owners of this retreat. From the outside, the late-eighteenth-century dwelling looks like many others on the pine-dappled coastline of Maine. Step inside, however, and you are at once struck by the joyful energy of the interior. Color and texture are skillfully layered in every corner of the house, resulting in an atmosphere that exudes confidence and a healthy sense of humor. To say that a vibrant color scheme is the common thread that binds all rooms in this house only begins to describe the decor. True, strong, saturated hues are evident in every part of the house, but they are rarely used in the same way twice. In one room it is the walls that wear the color; in another, walls are left white while the floors are painted a bold red or a sunny yellow. In rooms where white walls and plain pine floors appear as traditional as they come, splashes of color are supplied by the furnishings—a grass-green sofa, for instance, or a cornflower-blue table. By varying the use of color, the owners have created a sense of anticipation for visitors; guests never know what might greet them around the next corner.

New and vintage furnishings throughout the house share a common functionality, sturdiness, and practicality. All can withstand daily use by adults, children, and pets. A plus, too, for cottages set by oceans or lakes where wet bathing suits and sand-covered flip-flops are par for the course in warm weather. Color is again called on to make these functional furnishings a little

more fun. Coated with glossy shades of yellow, blue, or red, even the most sensible tables and chairs seem to smile. Slipcovers are also a frequent sight in the cottage, transforming upholstered pieces into solid-color fields. What's more, the easy-care nature of slipcovers allows the owners to be carefree about spills and scuff marks.

Plenty of shelves were a must for this family, who love to display their collections for all to see and enjoy. When occupying open shelves, vintage vases, teapots, and kitchenware can be viewed by visitors and are also easily accessible when dinnertime rolls around. (The owners feel strongly that using collections on a regular basis is one of the best ways to honor them.) Other collections, such as seashells and beach stones prominently positioned in a room, showcase the

ABOVE: AN ANTIQUE TRESTLE TABLE set in front of a sunny window becomes an ideal work space for this cottage's creative owner. Cubbies are great accessories for studios and home offices because they can hold art supplies, sketch pads, and reference books in an orderly fashion. Vintage vases are ideal receptacles for pens, pencils, and paintbrushes.

TOP RIGHT: A PANELED BED FRAME was chosen to echo the whitewashed walls of this sunny bedroom. Bursts of tomato red on the bedside table, armchair, and bedspread set against the sunflower-yellow floors move the eye around the room. Although its scale is smaller than the bed, the two-tiered bench's usefulness makes it a vital element in the room. The space beneath a window is an unexpected yet fun place to hang a painting.

RIGHT: APPROPRIATELY, the garden of this color-filled cottage is also alive with bold hues: red, green, yellow, pink. Glossy red paint unifies two pairs of garden chairs. New cedar siding gave the late-1700s structure a face-lift.

ABOVE: *IN THE KITCHEN*, two new yellow chairs and two vintage plank-seat chairs become an unlikely yet attractive set around the table. Red paint on the floors complements the exposed brick behind the wood stove. If you've got a creative eye as this owner does, try your hand at decorative touches around the room, such as the painted finish on the grandfather clock behind the door and the found-object sculptures on the wall.

artistry of the natural world. In most rooms, windows are kept unencumbered by curtains, letting in light and garden views but never detracting from the collections and furnishings of a room.

Have these photographs whet your appetite for color? If so, take some cues from this cottage when choosing your personal palette. To find the colors that best express who you are and what you love, look around you. These owners found inspiration in the natural

world outside their door (sea blue, spruce green, ripe-tomato red, sunflower yellow, seashell pink) and in the collections that line their shelves (mid-1900s pottery, whimsical painted-wood sculptures). To determine what colors are right for you, look to your collections. Are your cupboards filled with yellowware? Blue-and-white porcelain? Cranberry glass? You might also find the colors of your dreams in the garden or in your wardrobe. Remember that the hues you choose should reflect your taste, not what other people think is "proper" for a house. Tangerine may not be everyone's cup of tea, but if it's yours, have fun with it. Your enthusiasm will be infectious.

Once you've found a palette that you respond to, consider how you want to use it in your house. Walls are not the only place color can be concentrated. As you can see in these photographs, woodwork, floors, and furnishings are all great places to enliven with paint, wallpaper, or fabric. It's wise to keep your scheme to one or two dominant colors—in this home, green and yellow dominate the family's common room while yellow and red were chosen for a bedroom beneath the eaves. Limiting your combinations will prevent bold hues from overwhelming small spaces.

ABOVE: *OPEN METAL SHELVING*—a style often seen in restaurants—is great for displaying collections in the kitchen. Here, colorful mid-twentieth-century teapots and vases congregate with cookbooks, family photos, and a trusted family friend: the toaster oven. Most home-improvement stores and mail-order catalogues devoted to kitchenware carry similar shelving. If pets and small children are everyday occupants of your house, cluster collections on the higher shelves.

5

Details

Two cottage rooms may be similar in many ways:

They may both have white walls, white slipcovered furnishings, and whitewashed shutters on the windows. What will set them apart, however, will be the collections, the artwork, and the countless details that personalize a home and mark it, unmistakably, as the dwelling of its owner. Imagine that one homeowner were an avid gardener. She might place miniature topiaries along the mantel in her all-white room, hang framed botanical prints above the sofa, and lay a floral motif hooked rug underfoot. A collector of contemporary glass, on the other hand, might line her mantel with colorful Murano vases; opt for playful watercolors in bright blues, yellows, and reds on the walls; and choose a royal-blue carpet for the floor. Though the backgrounds in each room are the same, the end results are as different as can be. Once you've covered the basics in your home, here are some distinguishing details to consider.

Displaying Collections

The objects we choose to surround ourselves with say a lot about who we are, revealing clues to our pastimes and our passions. Arranged in the home, collections not only help visitors understand their hosts a little better, they often spark conversations. When collections grow large, as they are wont to do, it's not always easy to determine where to put them or how to pare them down. There's a tendency to want to show everything at once, when selecting a few favorite pieces—and rotating others in and out of the arrangement—might make a greater visual impact. For sizable collections, it can be helpful to designate an area just for them, like a cupboard, curio cabinet, or book-case. Large collections can also be displayed in small clusters around the house: A person with an eye for roses, for example, might fill a dining room cupboard with rose-pattern china, line a living room shelf with rose still lifes, and hang a row of vintage hats brimming with silk roses from a peg rail in the bedroom or foyer.

RIGHT: *Several techniques for displaying collections* can be found in this photograph. In the kitchen, a cupboard has been designated the showcase for a lively group of enamelware coffee- and teapots. Choosing just a few for each shelf highlights the subtleties of each design. The wall space above a doorway is a great place to hang long narrow items, such as the train depot sign shown here; panoramic photographs and vintage vacation banners would also work well. Plates hung on the wall in the dining area create a pleasing (and space-appropriate) arrangement.

LEFT: *There are many advantages* to displaying collections along a high shelf. For one thing, fragile or valuable items can be kept out of reach of children, pets, and curious hands. Second, a single long row highlights subtle differences between objects. Finally, the shelf and its contents become an eye-catching wall decoration in the room.

ABOVE: *Old garden ladders are lovely places* to display textiles. In this photograph, one is used as a casual quilt rack for early-1900s redwork quilts. They can also hold collectible dishtowels in the kitchen, plush bath towels in the bathroom, and warm camp blankets in the guest room.

BELOW: *LARGE COLLECTIONS* look especially eye-catching when grouped together. To avoid overwhelming small spaces with sizable groups of objects, devote an entire bookcase or cupboard to their display. Vintage seashell crafts like these would complement a seaside house particularly well, though they could also keep the spirit of summer alive year-round in any region of the country.

ABOVE: *EMPTYING A FEW SHELVES* in a bookcase creates an ideal place to display prized possessions. When positioning fragile pieces, such as this collection of pink lusterware, clear away all books and devote the entire shelf to the collection. Sturdier objects such as cast-iron doorstops, on the other hand, can share shelf space with books without much fear that a leaning volume will cause significant damage.

RIGHT: *By ORGANIZING* a large collection of 1920s celluloid cold-cream jars, cotton-ball dispensers, and jewelry cases into neat rows the look is kept clean and uncluttered. A framed star-pattern crib quilt and framed botanical prints make a dramatic wall display in the bedroom across the hall.

Filling Wall Space

When looking for the perfect wall decorations for your home, expand your search by seeing beyond traditional paintings, photographs, and prints. Salvaged architectural elements—such as wrought-iron fencing, tin ceiling tile, or gingerbread woodwork—are another category whose sculptural qualities become evident when hung on the wall. Wide expanses of wall space—over a sofa, mantel, sideboard, or headboard—can be the most challenging to fill. The easiest way to handle these spaces is with a single eye-catching work, such as a painting, trade sign, or travel poster. A series of botanical prints or framed quilt blocks can also be called upon to fill sizable spaces, as can a group of family photographs in frames of various sizes and styles. Narrow columns between windows and doorframes can be filled with a single vertical item or a series of small frames, plates, porcelain wall pocket vases, or decorative trivets hung one above the other.

BELOW: *DISPLAYED ON THE WALL*, a small section of wrought-iron fencing becomes a piece of
sculpture. The salvaged garden element is especially fitting in this setting, where a patio table
has been positioned beside a chaise longue and
fresh flowers abound. Many styles of fencing can
be found to fit just about any decor, from highly
ornamental to sleek and modern.

OPPOSITE: *IN THIS DINING ROOM*, five plates
from a large ironstone collection form a
graceful arch above a sideboard. The other
items displayed on the sideboard were carefully chosen to hint at the breadth of the
collection, most of which is stored behind
the cupboard's doors.

ABOVE: *A SINGLE STRIKING PAINTING* can
become the focal point of an entire room.
Floral still lifes like this one from the 1930s
are ideal for cottage homes. Similar images
can frequently be found at flea markets and
antiques malls. Placing a flower-print pillow on the bed creates a pleasing counter-
point to the art on the wall.

ABOVE: *PANTRIES AND MUDROOMS* can accommodate a large number of kitchen necessities when lined floor to ceiling with open shelves. Gently curving supports add a graceful touch to the utilitarian shelves. Embellishing a pantry door with a chalkboard surface creates a useful spot for shopping lists and children's drawings.

BELOW: *A CONSISTENT STYLE OF PLACE-MENT* brings an artistic touch to everyday objects. In this photograph, each shelf holds a platter or two set behind a row of pitchers or canisters. Feel free to mix old and new in an arrangement if they share a similar look: The new canisters on the bottom shelf look right at home with the antique ironstone that surrounds them. If a cupboard doesn't already have them, grooves can be cut into shelves to help stabilize the plates and platters on display.

Storage Solutions

Many cottage homes lack ample storage for collections and everyday items. Wire-rack systems (available at home-improvement stores) and other organizers help make use of every inch of space in closets and cabinets. When closet space is exhausted, creative solutions can be devised throughout the house. Armoires can be transformed into entertainment centers in living rooms and dens, into extra closets in bedrooms, and into pantries for dry goods and glassware in kitchens. Baskets are another attractive alternative: In the living room they can hold firewood, magazines, or warm throws; in the bedroom, extra blankets, sewing supplies, or favorite novels; in the bathroom, towels, washcloths, and toiletries. Selecting furnishings that serve dual purposes can also be a big help: A blanket chest positioned in front of a sofa, for example, becomes both coffee table and additional storage for board games, videos, DVDs, and photo albums.

ABOVE: *TAKEN OUT OF THE DINING ROOM*, large cupboards can serve myriad purposes elsewhere in the house. In this pared-down bedroom, a tall cupboard holds bed linens and towels. When storing items in glass-front cupboards, be mindful of what things you put on upper shelves and how you arrange them. Sweaters or dungarees might be better suited for storage in the cabinet down below; collections or household linens that can be artfully arranged look best behind the glass doors.

BELOW: *SPACIOUS DINING ROOM CUPBOARDS* expand storage space for dinnerware, linens, and other collections. Styles can match a room's existing furnishings, such as the weathered cupboard and table seen here. A long basket set atop the cupboard serves both practical and decorative purposes in the room; it can hold additional linens or simply be left empty to reflect the white-painted finish of the chairs and table base below.

ABOVE: *CUSTOM-BUILT CUBBIES* with space for baskets and peg rails are especially good for mudrooms and entryways. Store umbrellas, hats, and scarves in the baskets. A large cubby in the center can be used as a seat for changing muddy boots or sandy flip-flops. A similar wall unit would also be a welcome addition in the laundry room (to house an iron, detergent, spray starch, and other items) or a kid's room (to organize toys, clothes, and childhood sundries).

Cupboards

The perfect cupboard, prominently positioned, can instantly impart cottage style to any room in the house. Of course, the exact size, style, and color of each person's "perfect" cupboard will vary greatly. Fortunately, countless designs were constructed over the past two centuries to accommodate almost every taste. Perhaps your ideal design is a blue-painted pie cupboard from the 1800s that you discovered in an antiques shop. Or maybe it's a sturdy pine hutch with open shelves above and a spacious cabinet below that you spotted in a catalogue. You may have inherited your grandmother's 1930s mahogany breakfront as part of her dining room set. If unsure of your ideal match, browse through decorating magazines and home-design books for inspiration. Once you've found your heart's desire, the next step will be deciding where to place it and what items to store in it. The dining room has always been the most common location for large freestanding cupboards. In the nineteenth and early-twentieth centuries, they served as both storage and display space for a family's everyday wares and precious heirlooms: pottery, glassware, pewter, and the like. Dining room cupboards are still frequently found in cottage interiors today. On their shelves, sets of china with decorative motifs and treasured collections are now interspersed with personal mementos such as family photos, children's crafts, and vacation souvenirs, creating a scrapbook of sorts about its owner's life. Breaking with tradition, cupboards originally intended for the dining room have also been making appearances in other parts of the house. In the living room pictured here, for instance, an antique corner cupboard not only protects a few artfully placed possessions, it adds a burst of color to the room as well. A glass-front cupboard placed in a bedroom could hold family photographs in silver frames on its upper shelves and warm blankets in the cabinet below; in the bathroom, it could be towels and washcloths above and bars of soap, rolls of toilet tissue, and cleaning supplies below. Although many designs are attractive exactly as they are, many people enjoy embellishing cupboards with decorative treatments such as patterned drawer liners or scalloped paper edging along the end of each shelf. Decals or stenciled designs can be applied to cupboard doors, a popular option when the furnishings are used in children's rooms. Applying wallpaper in a pretty floral print to the interior of a solid-door cupboard presents a lovely surprise each time you go to retrieve a plate, platter, or whatever you may have stored inside.

ABOVE: ROOMY CUPBOARDS with wonderful painted finishes are eagerly sought for cottage homes. Once a large cupboard has reached its full storage capacity, a collection of baskets in various shapes and sizes can be used to accommodate additional objects. Single wooden side chairs and small tables are common sights at flea markets; paired together in a setting like this—where each piece of furniture has a style all its own—makes even mismatched items seem like a perfect fit.

Flea-Market Style

Flea markets are great places to uncover collectibles, storage units, and one-of-a-kind furnishings for the home—nearly all at bargain prices, making these sales ideal for anyone decorating on a budget. The secret to successful flea-market decorating is learning to spot potential when perusing a sale. Anyone who's been to a flea market even once knows that the furniture and accessories found there are rarely in perfect condition. More often than not they have a slight scuff here and there or they are missing a leg or a drawer pull. If you can train your eye to see the graceful curves hidden beneath layers of unattractive paint, you'll master this style of decorating in no time. Add to this the ability to think up new uses for old objects (garden benches as coffee tables, medicine bottles as bud vases, for example), and you're home free. Having a single color scheme to search for can also make flea-market shopping a bit easier: If you know you're looking for only white wares —or items that can easily be whitewashed—you can keep an eye out for just those things and overlook much of the jumble found at these sales.

ABOVE: *TRANSFORMING IMPERFECT OBJECTS* into useful household accessories is one of the best parts of flea-market decorating. In this sitting room, vintage quilts with concentrated damage on the edges were salvaged and used as upholstery fabric for the wing chairs. (Smaller sections from a severely damaged quilt could top an ottoman or footstool.) Another tip: Always look beyond an item's painted finish. Small tables and lamp stands can be repainted in any shade that will complement their new setting, in this case, green and fuchsia.

DECORATING WITH ARCHITECTURAL SALVAGE

There are two ways to incorporate architectural elements into the cottage interior: Place them where they were originally intended (a stained-glass transom above a front door, for example) or invent a new use (a stained-glass transom hung on the wall as a work of art). Flea markets are a good source of architectural salvage, or check the yellow pages to find salvage sources near you.

Home Offices

As working from home becomes an
option more and more people are
taking advantage of, home offices
have become a desirable detail even
in the coziest of cottages. Fortunately, you don't need to devote an
entire room to the project to create
a pleasant, efficient work space. In
many cottages, extra bedrooms serve
double duty as guest room and home
office. In cases such as this, you can
make the room less "bedroom" and
more "office" by choosing a daybed
that functions as a sofa until guests
arrive. Garden rooms or enclosed
porches are other spots to consider
for a work space (wicker or
wrought-iron tables and chairs work
especially well in these settings).
Even a small corner of the kitchen
can be utilized. Following the
trend, home-design catalogues and
home-improvement stores now
feature a wide variety of space-
saving supplies for the home office,
such as hanging files hidden in
rustic baskets and roomy armoires
that can easily accommodate a com-
puter, printer, and fax machine.

BELOW: *You don't need* lots of space to create an office area in your home. Open shelves can hold reference books and extra reams of paper; Gothic arches make the shelves in this photograph a bit out of the ordinary. Laptop computers are good bets in small houses, as they can easily transform even a narrow ledge into an efficient work surface. Vintage vases, plant stands, and letter slots are handy organizational aids for pens, paper clips, envelopes, and the like.

OPPOSITE: *This homeowner* simply tucked a table and chair into a light-filled corner and called it her office. Once the location is settled, the home office requires little else besides a desk large enough to suit your needs and a comfortable chair. Files or additional materials can be neatly stowed in a nearby closet or cupboard.

ABOVE: *Filled with light* on sunny days, garden rooms and enclosed porches are ideal spots for home offices. A wicker desk was made more businesslike with the addition of a wooden cubby unit that holds stationery and other office essentials. Wicker porch furniture creates a setting that would be ideal for any profession that requires meeting with clients in the home. Hand-painted signs relating to work, such as the one mounted above the desk, are fun accessories for home offices, and the chandelier adds a pretty touch of whimsy.

Porches

Over the years, these outdoor
"rooms" have become some of the
most beloved spots in the cottage
home, and their decoration often
receives the same level of attention
as the rest of the house. Floorboards
are lovingly painted; chairs and
cushion fabrics carefully chosen;
and hanging flower baskets lushly
planted. Porch furnishings vary in
style and include ornate wicker
settees, rustic bent-twig rockers,
and wrought-iron tables with gleaming glass tops. Front porches should
always be ready to welcome friends,
family, and first-time visitors.
An uncluttered look—a pair of
comfortable rockers and a small table
on which to rest cool drinks, for
example—works best here. Because
a back or side porch tends to be
more private, this is the place for
hammocks, picnic tables, baskets
filled with board games, and items
of a personal nature. If the design of
your porch (and the size of your
budget) allows, it might be worth
considering glass windows that can
enclose the space in the winter,
making the porch a room you can
use year-round.

OPPOSITE: *A FRONT OR SIDE PORCH* doesn't need much to be cheerful and welcoming. Folding chairs are good to keep on hand; additional seats can be brought out when visitors arrive and are easy to store when not in use. Here, a glossy coat of barely-blue paint enlivens the floor, steps, and ceiling. A potted hydrangea and a climbing rose blur the line between garden and porch, enhancing both.

BELOW: *Sliding doors that can be opened* in the summer and tightly closed in the winter are a desirable detail of this cottage's dining area. The doors, along with the garden chairs and the weathered potting table that make up the dining room suite, underline the setting's proximity to the garden.

ABOVE: *Colorful blooms and garden furnishings*, such as a painted bench, rooster-and-hen statuary, bee skep, and porch chairs, populate this cheerful garden. Trellises (available at home-improvement stores) are classically cottage elements, especially when climbing roses, morning glories, or other flowering vines are allowed to thrive. The peg rail hung beside the door displays a Frisbee and a collection of vintage buoys, but would be equally useful for dog leashes, hats, and light jackets.

Cottage Gardens

As long as there have been cottages, there have been cottage gardens—plots that exude the same carefree, irreverent style as the rooms within. Historically, a cottage's front garden would have featured a straight path leading from the street to the front door, flanked on both sides by exuberant plantings of old-fashioned flowers—phlox, hollyhocks, daisies, delphiniums, foxgloves. Garden plots at the back of the house often incorporated herbs and vegetables, bee skeps, chicken coops, fruit trees, and storage sheds. Today most cottage gardens—both front and back—resemble the front gardens of old: Heavy hydrangea blossoms add bursts of blue, pink, and white; climbing roses adorn trellises and porch columns; and lavender wands and cheerful daisies line winding brick paths. Books about cottage gardens will help you determine what plant and flower varieties grow best in your region of the country. Dozens of volumes have been written on the subject. To find one, check the gardening section of your local bookstore or library.

Like any room in the cottage home, cottage gardens are generally outfitted with "furnishings" all their own. Wrought-iron garden benches or rustic bent-twig table-and-chair sets, for example, are commonly placed amid the greenery, providing a quiet spot to meditate in the afternoon. Trellises and arbors are essential elements as well, providing an ideal home for climbing roses. Birdhouses and garden statuary, such as cement turtles or bronze bunnies, add a whimsical touch to the scene. To instill your yards with instant old-fashioned flavor, seek out vintage garden accessories such as birdhouses, trellises, and garden benches at flea markets and garden-antiques shows. Although chicken coops and bee skeps are rare sights in most gardens today, small wooden structures that can double as a storage facility and potting shed are popular and can be found through home-improvement stores. Painted sheds—red with white trim or white with black trim, for instance—look especially charming in the cottage garden.

City dwellers need not lament their lack of acreage: The spirit of a cottage garden can dwell on a small terrace, in a window box, even along a sunny windowsill. Potted flowers and herbs, rustic birdhouses, even small trellises can be called upon in these situations. In addition to consulting a book on cottage gardens, peruse a volume on indoor gardening or potted gardens to discover which classic cottage blooms will thrive indoors or in small containers.

RIGHT: *THE ARTFULLY ARRANGED GARDEN* can easily become one of the places you spend the most time. Trellises, picket fencing, and birdhouses are all classically cottage; garden furniture can be given a whimsical look when painted to match an owner's favorite flowers, like the pink bentwood chair near the umbrella shown here. Potted plants extend nature's bounty beyond the garden's border.

LEFT: *PORCHES CAN BE DECORATED* like any other room in the house: They can be filled with the furnishings, collections, and accessories you love most. They can also be given a pared-down look or a style that is over the top. This owner's passion for red and green is evident in the red geraniums, the fabrics cushioning the wicker settees, the wire birdcage, and the transferware plates on the porch post. A sunshade held in place with plaid ribbon can be let down on bright afternoons.

BELOW: *THE IDEAL COTTAGE GARDEN* is not one with ordered rows and painstakingly designed plantings. It is one of exuberant layering of color and texture and of plants growing any which way they can, whether spilling over a border or climbing the trunk of a tree. Shelves installed beneath the windows of this charming red-and-green cottage support flowerpots large and small, all filled with impatiens.

ABOVE: *BEDROOMS THAT OPEN ONTO THE GARDEN* are charming oases. Potted impatiens and geraniums bring the blooms right up to the door. Fresh-flower arrangements, floral-motif curtains, and a delicate needlepoint pillow continue the garden theme indoors. Placing a small woven mat inside the door keeps dirt from being tracked through the house. At night, the door's screened window lets in cool breezes and the sounds of crickets.

BELOW: *Daybeds are great porch accessories* for both lively gatherings and restful afternoon naps. A trundle ensures extra space for large groups. On screened porches, the beds can even be used for outdoor sleeping on warm nights. A collection of vintage-fabric pillows in reds and greens complements the soft green of the bed frame.

ABOVE: *In warm weather*, a screened porch often becomes a family's favorite place to dine. It will be used so often that a separate table and chairs for the porch are a wise investment. If on a budget, peruse thrift shops and flea markets for casual furnishings. A fresh coat of paint will spruce up anything exhibiting too much wear and tear. Dress the table with cheerful linens and vintage dinnerware, such as the Jade-ite plates and striped tumblers seen here. A garden bouquet arranged in a transferware pitcher provides the perfect finishing touch.

ABOVE: *CAREFULLY PLACED IN AN ALL-WHITE SETTING*, even the most common household accessories look like works of art. The sculptural qualities of these vintage ironstone mixing bowls became apparent when they were displayed beside a window. Countless everyday items, such as cobalt medicine bottles, wire baskets, and even wooden potato mashers, can be used to create artful arrangements.

OPPOSITE: *REMOVING NONSTRUCTURAL WALLS* created a single large room that incorporates living, dining, and cooking areas. White walls, woodwork, and furnishings create a cohesive look throughout. Items originally intended for outdoor use look great in cottage interiors; here, garden chairs surround the dinner table, sap buckets hold potted plants on the mantel, and a cement urn stores firewood by the hearth.

A Cottage Furnished with Flea-Market Finds

Treasures—and great ideas—abound in the airy interior of this Southern California bungalow. Not surprising once you know that the owners are well versed in the art of flea-market decorating. For one thing, they know how to spot potential amid the maze of a market. The living room mantel—though the perfect design for the period of their new house—was too narrow for the hearth, but with a carpenter's aid, it could be easily widened to fit the space. The owners also knew how to find new uses for old things (garden furniture was brought indoors, framed fabric remnants became works of art, tin buckets were used as vases and flowerpots). But before they could even consider where to position the sofa or which kind of chairs to use in the dining area, the structure itself—a 1920s Arts and Crafts design—needed a face-lift.

Because the original floor plan featured a series of small dark rooms, the owners began by removing nonstructural walls and adding windows to create a sunny, open living/dining/cooking area. An addition was also added to the back of the house to accommodate a spacious master bedroom. When the layout was finalized, a color scheme was chosen for the entire house. Except for floors and details in varying types of wood, crisp white was used for everything from walls and woodwork to furnishings and accessories. The all-white interior visually expands the small space and allows even large pieces like the sofa to seem perfectly proportioned. Walls, windows, and floors are kept clean and free of excessive decoration—a single photograph or framed print appears when needed, a shade or gauzy curtain where privacy is wanted, and small rugs beside beds and bathtubs.

LEFT: WHEN THE OWNERS' DREAM MANTEL turned out to be too narrow for the hearth, they commissioned a carpenter to widen it. The cupboards flanking the fireplace were built from salvaged wood, giving them an authentic old-fashioned look. Frequently seen at flea markets, small tables and trunks like these can be used in myriad ways around the house.

Although the area allotted to the "living room" was compact, the owners were able to make two distinct seating areas by positioning a large sofa against the wall opposite the fireplace and two overstuffed armchairs between the sofa and the fireplace. Facing the sofa, the armchairs comfortably seat larger groups; facing the fireplace, the armchairs are ideal for intimate tête-à-têtes. All the upholstered pieces wear white slipcovers to blend in with the decor.

The "dining room" was confined to the area in front of a bay window, but a simple dark wood trestle table surrounded by four whitewashed garden chairs were all the small space required to make it look as elegant as a full room. A wide counter divides the dining and kitchen areas. Topped with butcher block and sided with salvaged beaded board, the custom-built

RIGHT: *BUTCHER-BLOCK COUNTERTOPS* ensure plenty of work space in a small kitchen. Although salvaged windows are great for cabinet doors, large numbers of matching windows can be difficult to find. Let dealers or salvage sources know what you are searching for; most will keep an eye out for specific designs and call when they locate them.

kitchen cabinets look as if they were original to the house. Salvaged windows were used on the upper cabinets—a fresh twist on glass-front cabinet doors.

Both bedrooms in the cottage reflect the same serene color scheme found elsewhere in the house. The smaller guest bedroom doubles as an office; piled high with fluffy pillows, the iron-framed daybed is a cozy spot for reading. A charming four-poster dominates the master bedroom. Off the master bedroom, the master bath harbors wonderful flea-market finds, including a classic claw-foot tub and twin antique sinks that were in such good condition that refinishing was unnecessary. Even the garden was decorated with flea-market finds. French bistro chairs, a whitewashed potting table, salvaged trellises, and an antique watering can populate the verdant plot that overflows with flowers and plants.

A COTTAGE FURNISHED WITH FLEA-MARKET FINDS ❧ 141

ABOVE: *AS THE MASTER BEDROOM'S* four-poster and whitewashed footed cupboard illustrate, small bedrooms need little more in the way of furnishings than a stunning bed frame and a charming nightstand. Salvaged windows and floorboards make the room—located in a new addition—look as if it were always part of the original house. A framed Victorian print hung over the bed is both simple and dramatic.

LEFT: *THE MASTER BATHROOM'S CLAW-FOOT TUB* and matching antique sinks were flea-market finds. The tub was outfitted with a brass shower-curtain frame; the sinks were set into a custom-built cabinet. Large squares of tin ceiling tile were used as frames for the matching mirrors above the his-and-her sinks. A butcher-block top and beaded-board siding visually link this cabinet to those found in the kitchen. Small hanging shelves are great places to keep hand towels, washcloths, and a potted plant.

RIGHT: *A CAST-IRON TWIN-BED FRAME* becomes a daybed in the guest room. A voluptuous pile of pillows beckons family and friends to curl up with a cup of tea and a good book. An iron candelabra makes an unexpected bedside light. When framed, vintage toile looks like a wonderful work of art whose proportions perfectly fit the space above the bed.

Top a bedside table with a decorative-edged doily.

Use straw hats as decorative elements in the house.

Store plates in an open rack in the kitchen.

Install a high shelf above the windows to use for storage and display.

Line linen closet shelves with delicate paper edging.

Paint a checkerboard pattern on the floor.

Use large baskets to store extra quilts, pillows, or warm throws.

Use upholstered ottomans and foot-stools as small tables or extra seating.

Position a comfortable chair beside a sunny window.

Place a weathered garden bench beside a sunny window.

Set a table in the garden and eat lunch outdoors.

Group family photographs alongside a staircase.

Transform canning jars into flower vases.

Lay a classical country rug on
the floor.

Color coordinate collections with
shades of paint.

Add a decorative trim
to shelves.

Trim the tops of windows
with lace valances.

Paint a hardwood floor a bright color.

Use vintage picnic tins as storage for dry goods, napkins, and other kitchenware.

Keep bars of soap in a milk-glass compote in the bathroom.

Make pillows out of vintage tablecloths.

Install rounded corner shelves to display favorite collections.

Arrange antique watering cans along a bench or shelf.

Keep a picnic basket close at hand for impromptu outings.

Mount a hand-painted trade sign on the wall.

Photography Credits

Index